BEANS

Four Principles for Running a Business in Good Times or Bad

A Business Fable Taken From Real Life

~ ~

Leslie A. Yerkes

Charles Decker

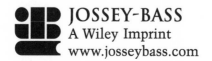

JOSSEY-BASS
A Wiley Imprint
www.josseybass.com

Published by Jossey-Bass
A Wiley Imprint
989 Market Street, San Francisco, CA 94103-1741
www.josseybass.com

Jossey-Bass books and products are available through most bookstores. To contact Jossey-Bass directly call our Customer Care Department within the U.S. at 800-956-7739, outside the U.S. at 317-572-3986, or fax 317-572-4002.

Jossey-Bass also publishes its books in a variety of electronic formats. Some content that appears in print may not be available in electronic books.

Library of Congress Cataloging-in-Publication Data

Yerkes, Leslie, 1958–
    Beans : four principles for running a business in good times or bad : a business fable taken from real life / by Leslie A. Yerkes and Charles Decker.—1st ed.
        p. cm.
    ISBN 0-7879-6764-5 (alk. paper)
    1. Small business—United States—Management. 2. Customer services—United States. 3. Quality of products—United States. 4. Employee morale—United States. I. Decker, Charles, 1952– II. Title.
    HD62.7.Y47 2002
    658.02'2—dc21

                                                        2003006449

Printed in the United States of America
FIRST EDITION

HB Printing   10 9 8 7 6 5 4 3 2 1

Contents

Foreword *xi*
          Bob Nelson

Preface *xv*

Authors' Note *xix*

Introduction *1*

1   PASSION: You gotta have it
           or you gotta get it   7

2   PEOPLE: You're known by
           the company you keep   19

3   MAKE IT PERSONAL:
           Everybody wants to be a regular   34

~ Contents ~

4   PRODUCT: People don't pay good money for bad coffee 61

5   THE EYE OF INTENTION: If you don't know where you're going, you won't know when you get there 72

6   THE FOUR P'S: Big lessons from a small cup of coffee 87

Epilogue: SIX WEEKS LATER 111

A Page From Carol Wisdom's Notes 119
Discussion Questions: Applying the Four P's to Your Work Experiences 123
Appendix: Caffeine Facts 137
Acknowledgments 145
About the Authors 149
Contact Page 153

To our wonderfully supportive families

Foreword

This is a true story about The El Espresso coffee shop. Although the real-life coffee shop goes by another name, this small business is typical of many other businesses, large and small, that operate every day across America and around the world. The El Espresso has chosen to stay small and do what it does best: serve its customers well.

In this age of headlines about corporate executives run amok, Jack and Dianne Hartman, the owners of The El Espresso, are the kind of businesspeople who deserve a little good press. For more than twenty years, they have stayed true to their values and their principles. In the process, they have created a business that has earned the reputation for serving Seattle's best coffee—coffee good enough to make people willing to line up in the rain to buy a cup.

I work with thousands of managers and business owners every year, most of them looking for ways to create a more successful business. The answer is simple: Hire the best people you can, allow them to be who they are, treat them fairly and reward them regularly, instill in them a love for serving the customers, and the customers will come back faithfully. These simple truths are the message of *Beans*.

To help you apply the principles of *Beans* to your own workplace, the book poses some great questions at the end, designed to help you examine the state of your own relationship with work— whether you are the owner, the manager, or an employee.

I invite you to read this short book and discover how these four principles for running a business in good times and bad might energize your employees, your customers, and quite possibly your entire organization.

As you read *Beans,* you will experience a business where everyone wants to be a regular, where the customer is known and respected, and there is an honest blur between serving people and running a business.

Learn the lessons of *Beans* and this can be your business, too.

April 2003
San Diego, California

Bob Nelson, Ph.D.
Author of *1001 Ways to Reward Employees* and *The 1001 Ways to Rewards and Recognition Fieldbook*

P.S. The authors have set up a great way to encourage feedback and interaction with their readers. Simply go to http://www.beansthebook.com and click on "Feedback." They would love to know how the simple lessons in this book resonate in your own organization.

Preface

It was a hot, late-summer day in Seattle during the first year of the new millennium. My friends Ken Blanchard and Harry Paul were taking me to lunch at the Seattle Public Market to celebrate the move of Harry's first book *(Fish!)* into the #1 slot at Amazon.com, where I worked.

Before lunch, we were planning to visit Pike Place Fish, home of the famous fish throwers depicted in Harry's book and video. As we walked down the street, we passed a tiny coffee counter with a long line of customers outside, cheerfully waiting

to get their lattes, espressos, and
cappuccinos. I pointed out the
store and the queue and said to
Ken, who is known far and wide
for his business case studies told
in parable and fable form, "There's
a story there." Intrigued, Ken asked
me to elaborate.

This is what I told him.

"Ken, every day, rain or shine, that place has a line
of customers waiting outside as long as twenty
minutes to get their coffee. In a downtown totally
dominated by Starbucks, Tully's, and Seattle's Best
Coffees, many of which have comfy sofas, fire-
places, and grand pianos, there has to be something special about this place. As you can see it's
only about twenty square feet with a ten-foot
counter and two tables for sitting outside in the
summertime. Yet it not only survives, it prospers.
And along the way it has created fantastic, fanati-
cal customer loyalty. There has to be some kind of
magic in a place to create that kind of customer
devotion.

"I think, Ken, from what I have observed, the key to this business's success is about the basics: Hire the best people you can, empower them, and instill in them a love of customer service. And when you follow the basics faithfully, you will be successful—whether you're a David competing against an army of Goliaths or you're in a division of a Fortune 500 company. It would make a great business story."

Ken said, "I totally agree. Why don't you write it?"

That wasn't the response I had been looking for. We continued on and had, as I recall, a truly great lunch.

More than a year after this conversation, my friend Leslie Yerkes, author of *Fun Works: Creating Places Where People Love to Work,* came to Seattle for several meetings, including one with some of my colleagues at Amazon.com. That night, as Leslie and I walked to dinner, I pointed out this inspirational organization

and I told her the same thing I had told Ken
Blanchard a year before. Two days later, Leslie
called me from Cleveland and said, "I've been
thinking about what you told me and I think
you're right: it *would* make a fantastic case study
for a book and a natural follow-up to *Fun Works*.
Why don't we collaborate?"

What you are about to read is that collaboration.
Leslie and I hope its inspiration will cause you
to contemplate the way you feel about your life,
about what you do, and how you act in good
times and bad.

It's our hope that *Beans* will help you brew up
success—cupful after cupful.

April 2003   Charles Decker
New York, New York

Authors' Note

This is a fictionalized account of a true story of real people running a real business. In the process of storytelling, as well as to protect the privacy of the people involved, names have been changed; some facts and situations are also the product of invention. The authors would like to thank those individuals who shared their recollections with us.

We believe strongly in the importance of group reading in companies and organizations. To help put these ideas into practice, at the end of the book you will find discussion questions designed to encourage conversation and commitment in companies large and small. To learn more about setting up a reading group in your own organization, go to our website

http://www.beansthebook.com

and click on "Business Literacy."

BEANS

Introduction

Beans is the story of The El Espresso, a company that has struggled and prospered in spite of intentionally staying small. *Beans* takes place in the heart of Seattle, the coffee capital of America. It's the story of a hole-in-the-wall David up against the corporate Goliaths on a daily basis. It's the story of Jack and Dianne Hartman and how they went from airline flight attendants to the king and queen of Seattle's espresso scene.

Beans is also the story of the people who have chosen to work for and patronize The El Espresso. You'll learn about what they brought to that

1

experience and what they got out of it. And you'll discover how The El Espresso has changed their lives and the lives of the Seattleites who consider the El their regular coffee stop.

Beans is the story of how The El Espresso does business. It is a story that seems to speak to a world responding to the changing face of business today. In reality, *Beans* is the story of a return to the old ways, when every sidewalk in New York had street vendors, when every town in Europe had a central market in which people sold their wares and services on a daily basis.

Beans shows us one way to survive in a world that's moving at the speed of light. It's a story that will demonstrate to each of us how to make our life and our business personal, passionate, and filled with people like us.

But mostly *Beans* is the story of how *Passion, People, Personal,* and *Product* can help you improve your work experiences whether you are an owner, a new manager, or an employee looking for a smarter way to work. And how the only way to successfully judge results is to look at them through what we call "The Eye of Intention."

The secret of *Beans* is that the quality of the cup of coffee, the quality of your work experience, is a direct result of what goes into making it. *Beans* will demonstrate clearly how each of us chooses every day what those ingredients will be, what proportion of each we will use that day, and how good a final product we will brew.

Along the way, *Beans* will ask you to stop and reflect about each of these P's and how they play out in your work:

Passion: Do you have passion for what you do? If not, why not? What could you do to find that passion and bring it with you each and every day? Do other people feel or experience your passion through your work? Can you sustain your passion over time?

People: What kind of people do you have working for you and with you? What kind of person are you? Are your customers the right ones? Have you been selective in choosing them and have you adequately prepared to serve them well? Have you created enduring relationships with those you serve and with whom you work?

Personal: Everybody wants to be a regular somewhere. Are you treating your customers like your friends? Do you know their names? The names of their family members? What they like to do when they're not at work? Can you say the same for your employees or coworkers? Do you make a meaningful connection with your customers and coworkers each and every day? Have you seen your efforts result in the creation of community?

Product: None of the other P's can save a bad product. Do you pay attention to the quality of what you make? What you serve? How you perform? Does your product represent who you are to the world? Have you created an environment where consistent product excellence can be sustained?

Like any story, *Beans* has a beginning, middle,
and an end. It has a back-story and an unknown
future. It is our hope that what you will learn
from *Beans* will help you to discover how to create
long-term success in your work and your life—
in good times or bad.

PASSION
You gotta have it
or you gotta get it

I have measured out my life in coffee spoons.
—T. S. Eliot, "The Love Song of J. Alfred Prufrock"

Bainbridge Island, Winslow, Washington
Across the Puget Sound from Seattle
5:55 A.M.

Jack Hartman rolls over and turns off the alarm five minutes before its scheduled 6 A.M. wake-up call. For years he has set an alarm only as a stopgap against the unlikely chance that he might sleep too long. Life is too much fun and too short

to sleep through it. When he was a flight atten-
dant for Continental Airlines, Jack never missed
a flight. In fact, he was almost always the first
crewmember to arrive for each day's airborne
adventure. Even though his "stewing" days are
long past, Jack is often still the first one up and
the first to arrive.

Without much thought, he performs his morning
ablutions—a quick shower and brushing of teeth.
Then he moves into the kitchen for his morning
cup of coffee, a ritual familiar to most of us yet one
that for Jack Hartman is entirely different. Jack's
morning cup comes not from a Mr. Coffee or a
spoon of instant in water boiled up in the micro-
wave. Jack's first tiny cup of the day is espresso—
thick, aromatic, and flavorful. A powerful elixir

of caffeine, flavor, and love made
with his highly polished stainless
steel King Coffee Espresso
machine—just a baby step below
the famous La Marzocco model
he uses all day long to satisfy the
caffeine cravings of hundreds
of customers at his Seattle business, The El Espresso.

Jack Hartman is known to many people as the King of Coffee, the man who made the espresso cart a common, everyday experience where thousands of Seattleites go every day to purchase their not-so-everyday cup of coffee. Every morning for twenty years, Jack has risen early and peddled his ten-speed Bianchi to work, *pulling* cups of espresso for the people of downtown Seattle. And every morning for the last twelve years, he has preceded that journey with thirty minutes of meditation.

Meditation is one of the ways in which Jack Hartman has simplified his life, using familiar phrases to screen out the cares of the world and bring peace to his being in preparation for facing a day filled with constant work and hundreds of customers. Making and keeping his life simple is one of his goals.

This morning, Dianne joins Jack at 6:45 for a quick good-morning and an espresso before she and her friends take off for a post-dawn rowing session in Puget Sound. Dianne Hartman has been Jack's partner in life as well as in business for those same twenty years. In true storybook fashion, Jack and Dianne met in mid-flight, in the galley of a DC-10, where they were both flight attendants preparing morning coffee for their passengers. The attraction was instant and natural, like cream and coffee. After several years in the air, Jack and Dianne decided to tie the knot and plant their feet on the ground when Jack bought a coffee-cart business called The El Espresso in downtown Seattle in 1980. Dianne likes to say that she's been serving coffee to people for thirty-five years: the first fourteen at thirty-five thousand feet and the next twenty-one at thirty-five feet above sea level in downtown Seattle.

For the last year or so, Dianne has been able to stay home or go rowing with friends or whatever she feels like because she has retired from the espresso business after twenty years as Jack's partner in the El. Though retired, she can't resist coming in several days a week to help out.

After Dianne's departure, Jack begins to pack up the El's famous chocolate chip cookies he baked last night. The cookies have become favorites of his customers, who would surely let

 him know their disappointment should he not have them available that day. Jack likes to say he's created a monster, but it's a monster that indicates how much his customers like him and the way he does business. It's a good monster to have.

Jack loads the cookies into his bike trailer and heads out on the four-mile journey through the hills of Bainbridge Island to the ferry dock.

Along the way, the twists and turns and ups and downs of the road make Jack think of the twists and turns and ups and downs of life that have placed him on a bucolic island across the Sound from Seattle, riding a bicycle on his way to the business he has created as much out of need as out of planning. Jack Hartman is one of those people who needed to start his own business to take full advantage of his passions in life— passion for coffee, for conversation, and for creating community. Jobs that fulfill those needs don't exist many places so it's often up to people like Jack to create them for themselves.

In 1979, Continental decided to pull out of its Seattle hub. As a result of Continental's decision to downsize, Jack and Dianne had a decision to make, too. If they wanted to keep their jobs as flight attendants, they would have to move to another city. If they didn't want to move, they would have to find new careers. It was a difficult decision because they loved how they made their living. But their love for Seattle turned out to be stronger than their love of flying. Besides, it wasn't the flying they loved so much as it was the people, the passengers. Now, all they had to do was find a people-centered job that would satisfy their passions.

As he heads down the hill to the Bainbridge Island ferry dock, Jack recalls his first entrepreneurial attempt following his time in the air— a floating bar called the Martini Barge in Lake Washington. He and some friends started the business mostly for something to do. And while it was modestly successful, Jack knew it wasn't a

career. As he sold drinks to customers, he found
that he loved being in business for himself. And
although he loved making people happy, he knew
something was wrong. Eventually he discovered
what that something was—he was selling a product he wasn't passionate about. He knew he
needed to make another change.

Years earlier, Jack had frequented a little place
called Cafe Allegro in the University District,
and he still remembered the joys of well-brewed,
well-pulled coffee. He recalled how energized he'd
feel after each cup. His time in the air had cen-
tered quite a bit around coffee, too. He knew
from both those experiences that a good cup of
coffee could go a long way toward making people

feel good, toward getting them
ready to take on the rest of the day.
So when the opportunity to purchase an established pushcart
business called The El Espresso
arose, Jack and Dianne raised
the $5,000 capital it required
and eagerly went into business
for themselves.

 The first section of Jack's daily bicycle journey ends as he arrives at the dock. His four-mile jaunt has energized him like a well-pulled espresso—blood is flowing to his brain and ideas are coming rapidly. He loads his gear aboard the ferry, secures it, and heads to the upper deck for the beautiful thirty-minute journey across Puget Sound.

As the ferry pulls away, the calming slap of water on the hull brings him back to thoughts of his journey through life with The El Espresso.

For the first three years of the business, Jack and Dianne devoted themselves to learning all they could about coffee. They applied the same passion they had in the air to creating and delivering the perfect cup of coffee. Soon, every cup they made was pulled with a passion that made it the best it could be. They soon discovered, however, that no matter how much passion they had for what they were doing, unless their clientele had a similar passion for coffee, they weren't going to stay in business for long. So rather than wait for their customers to develop that passion on their own, Jack and Dianne began to *create* it.

"Generating passion in your customers begins with teaching it every day," Jack always used to say. He'd said it to himself, to Dianne, to his employees, to anyone who would listen. And as much as he likes to talk, he realizes, that probably adds up to quite a few people.

"When you totally love what you make, it's just natural that your customers will love it, too," Jack had often thought as well. One of the first things he did to make people passionate about The El Espresso was to make every cup a double shot and sell it as a single. Jack thought that would be a good way to make his coffee twice as good as everybody else's. And it worked, he recalls, noticing that the ferry is already halfway to Seattle.

~ ~

As the ferry docks, the presence of Seattle's skyline looming over him makes Jack think about the reality he's been hiding from—things are not perfect at The El Espresso. His business does have some problems—with cash flow and with employees. These problems have begun to threaten his passion.

Additionally, the economy in general is down. Most of his loyal customers are still just that—loyal. But one of Seattle's largest employers, a dot-com with offices in the building next door to the El's countertop, has moved hundreds of employees, most of them loyal El customers, into new offices several miles away. And that has had a drastic impact on his business in two ways.

First, the top line has taken a deep hit. It will be difficult to replace hundreds of daily customers. Jack is certain it's theoretically possible to rebuild his customer base but he's unsure whether he has either the time or the heart for it anymore. Second, his employees are worried about

their future. (Hey, he's worried about his *own* future!) And when employees are worried, the customers soon know. Most pressingly, a key employee, George Guthrie, a man who's been pulling coffee with him for eight years and some-one Jack thinks the customers absolutely love, is showing signs of burnout. And that means Jack is going to have to have a heart-to-heart with George very soon. And, as much as he knows that's the right thing to do, he also knows it's going to be emotionally difficult for both of them. And that's not the part of the job he enjoys.

After much discussion with his best friend and partner, Dianne, Jack has decided to hire a business consultant to help him analyze the situation and devise new ways to build things up again. His great fear in this regard is that the recommendation might be to expand the business to meet increased competition from the chain coffee shops, as a previous consultant had suggested, with disastrous results. That's something he's definitely not interested in. For Jack Hartman, bigger is not better—it's just bigger.

At this moment, however, he has to get his bike up Spring Hill and prepare himself to deal with the new day, a ten o'clock meeting with what he has come to think of as his last resort—consultant Carol Wisdom—*and* do his best to overcome the funk he finds himself immersed in on this partly sunny day in Seattle

PEOPLE
You're known by the company you keep

The morning cup of coffee has an exhilaration about it which the cheering influence of the afternoon or evening cup cannot be expected to reproduce.
—Oliver Wendell Holmes, 1891

Pier 52
Seattle Harbor
8:00 A.M.

Getting around downtown Seattle would be a lot easier if it weren't for the hills, Jack thinks as he slowly peddles up Spring Hill in first gear. But if the hills weren't there, he wonders, would Seattle lose its charm? As is often the case for Jack Hartman, one conundrum conjures up another. A thought pops into his mind: wouldn't running a business be a lot easier, he wonders, if it weren't for the employees? But if the employees weren't there, would there be a business?

Like virtually everyone in today's workforce older than thirty, Jack grew up in a work culture that created and supported a love/hate relationship between companies and employees. It was like the old joke about men and women: you can't live with 'em and you can't live without 'em. The industrialized work-think of the last hundred years said that employees were a necessary evil—that every business would run much more smoothly if it weren't for the employees gumming up the works with their moods, their problems, and their needs. Fortunately, Jack has never really felt that way. To him, employees are the heart of his business—which is why this thought is so disturbing. The staff's variety of personalities is what makes a business unique.

The El Espresso is a living, breathing example of Jack's philosophy.

If it weren't for his employees, Jack knows he wouldn't be where he is today. And yet, lately he's become frustrated. He tries to push the thought out of his head as he points his Bianchi up one of the steeper roads he has to take to get to the El in downtown Seattle.

Pumping up Spring Hill is always difficult. As he gets older, Jack finds himself thinking more and more about getting off and walking up, but he doesn't. He stays the course and conquers this mountain every day, though recently it has seemed to be getting a little steeper. Well, he thinks, at least he no longer has to open; George Guthrie has been opening for the last several years. (And doing a pretty good job of it. If only his perform-ance the rest of the day maintained his early morning standard.)

And no longer does Jack have to be at the El every single minute, either. In point of fact, he no longer has to be there at all. Jack has quietly and simply changed the nature of The El Espresso from a job that he and Dianne shared into a business. It's a business, Jack muses, because of the employees—because they can operate The El Espresso successfully without him. That means he could sell the El should he choose. And while he is currently not interested in selling, it's a comfort to know he could. He takes solace in the fact that when it's time for him to make a change, the business will continue; his employees will not be without jobs nor his customers without their daily cup of coffee. And that freeing feeling makes the effort put out every day worth the aches and pains it causes him.

As he rounds the crest of the hill, he finds himself recalling many of the employees who've worked for The El Espresso.

Matt McMillian was his first employee, and an unlikely one because Matt is by nature an introvert—not all that fond of people, or so he says. But Matt stayed with Jack for nearly twenty years before he *retired.* During that time he learned the names and assorted factoids about thousands of customers—customers who kept coming back because of Matt. And the coffee, of course.

While Matt may claim not to need
to be around people all that
much, you couldn't tell it from
the ones he served. Last week
Matt stopped in to say "hey"
but spent the better part of his
twenty-minute stay being hugged by
customers who were glad to see him
again and repeatedly asked if he was
going to be coming back. Though he said no,
Jack could see a gleam in Matt's eyes that said he
missed pulling coffee and delighting customers
enough to give it some consideration.

Matt was the El's prime example of what Jack
thought of as "work is more than the money."
If having a job only meant taking home a paycheck, then Jack was sure anyone who had ever
worked for him could have done better somewhere else. But it's not. Work *is* more than the
money. It's about enjoying what you're doing.
It's about what you're doing being a natural
extension of yourself and fulfilling a need you
have. That's why Jack has always looked for
potential employees who first had passion and
second had the right attitude. He knew that if

people had both passion and the right attitude, then he could teach them the skills they'd need to pull a great cup of coffee. Matt was an example of that.

Maria Falsetto was another. Jack used to tease Maria that her name sounded like one of those they make up in books. But, bless her heart, that was her name. And there was nothing false about Maria. Maria was magic. Being around Maria was magic. She still says that working at the El was the most extraordinary work experience of her life. If so, Jack is sure Maria made it that way. He thinks that not only do people reflect their work environment but that every workplace reflects the people in it. Maria has often said that working at The El Espresso is like being a performance artist.

"The El is our stage, our space," she says. "Our customers float in and out of a continuing performance that's being judged every minute by everyone who stops by to get a cup of coffee from us. And as long as the performance is satisfying, predictable, yet constantly changing, our customers will return for repeat performances day after day after day."

Jack also likes to encourage his employees to engage the customers. He knows that when customers are connected to you, they are less willing to spend their money with a competitor. He knows that when employees know not only their customers' names but their families' names and what they do when they're not working, the customers develop such a strong relationship with the employees, the store, and the product that they feel as if they're being unfaithful when they buy a cup of coffee elsewhere. And it's not bad for business when customers feel that way. Not bad at all.

And yet, business was down. Particularly in the mornings, traditionally the busiest time. Was that a problem with his employees' not being connected to the customers? Or with not having enough customers in the first place? Or both? Jack had to find out.

~ ~

Pine Street and Fourth Avenue
Downtown Seattle
8:30 A.M.

As Jack pulls up to the hole in the wall that's known as The El Espresso, it looks like today will be a good day. The line is ten deep and George is wide awake and cheerful. He and Elizabeth Ortize are greeting arriving customers and talking with those in line, all the while pulling great cups of coffee with a pro-ficiency and speed that keeps customers satisfied while they chat in line with friends both old and brand new.

With George and Elizabeth handling the morning rush, Jack unpacks the cookies and reflects on how lucky he is to have employees who can handle the business without having to check with him on every detail. As he makes himself his second cup of the day, he thinks of Jim Howse, a customer who stopped by yesterday looking for another entrepreneur to commiserate with. Jim shows up every morning around the same time looking dead tired, before trudging over to the bar he owns on Third Avenue to open up at ten. He stays there until eight at night, leaving the duties of closing to his night manager. But he always returns at three in the morning, after closing, to check on his liquor inventory to make sure his employees aren't stealing anything or, worse, drinking the profits.

"We've got to keep a sharp watch on these guys or they'll steal us blind, eh, Jack?" Jim asked.

Jack was astounded when he heard that. "You get up and go back every night to count bottles and mark levels to see if they're stealing? I don't think life's worth that, Jim. If it were me, and here it *is* me, I just wouldn't do that."

"So what *do* you do? Let them take all your profits? Maybe you've got better margins than I do, but I can't leave anything to chance if I want to stay in business."

"Well, to each his own," Jack said with a shrug, "but here I hire good people and let them work."

"Let them work?" Jim asked incredulously. "Without supervision? How can you do that? Every day I give my manager a list of things I want done that day and every night she leaves that list with checkmarks by everything she's finished. What doesn't get done, I put on the next day's list. That way, nothing slips through the cracks."

"My philosophy is a little different, I guess," Jack said. "I trust my people to do the right thing. And then I don't sit around worrying that they won't. You know, trust really is stronger than fear; I tell my people what I expect—what our mission is— and we talk about goals for the week, the month, the year. We talk about the kind of money we can spend on improvement-type things, and then I let them alone. And not only do they take care of every single thing I would have put on a list, they come up with ideas of their own, often better than mine, and do them without asking. I like to think they consider the El as theirs and do the things they'd do if they really *did* own it."

"Well, Jack, you're a better man than I am. I just don't think I could do that. But I gotta say it sounds a whole lot more appealing than coming back every night at 3 A.M. to check on them. I'll have to think about what you've been saying."

Recalling his conversation with Jim almost makes Jack feel like he knows what he's doing. But if that were *really* true, then he wouldn't have needed to hire a consultant, would he? And he wouldn't have the problem he's having with George. Well, he'd have to deal with that one first, right after the morning rush.

Pine Street and Fourth Avenue
Downtown Seattle
9:30 A.M.

Since the lines at the El simply just got shorter or longer and never truly went away, it might be hard for some to imagine which hours of the day were the rush hours. But for Jack and his em-ployees, 9:30 was the beginning of a lull—they had thirty minutes before the mid-morning coffee-break crowd would make their way to Seattle's

29

streets in search of an invigorating cup of joe. So there was no way to put off talking to George any longer, he thought. Might as well get right to it.

Jack finds George where he always is this time of day, leaning against the back of the stand, a cup of decaf steaming in his hands. "Busy morning, eh, George?"

George grunts agreement, his eyes seemingly trying to divine some unknown truth hidden in the rising steam. So, Jack thinks to himself, George must realize that I know something's bothering him. I can always tell employees know I know something's wrong when they won't make eye contact.

This is going to be harder than it has to be. Certainly harder than he wants it to be.

"Have you noticed, George, that our morning rush isn't what it used to be?"

"Yeah, I have."

"And our morning receipts are down, too."

"That follows."

This really *is* going to be hard, Jack thinks. "And several of our morning regulars don't seem to stopping by anymore." Jack pauses, hoping George will pick up the conversation. All he gets from George, however, is silence. After a few uncomfortable moments, Jack continues. "I wonder if we need to take a look at our customer service?"

"Elizabeth and I are doing a good job. It's not us." George shifts slightly, his rigid stance projecting a defensive attitude.

"You know," Jack says, "sometimes when I'm not in the best of moods I can tell that I'm not doing my best with the customers. That ever happen to you?"

"I think our customer count is down because of the dot-coms moving out. You take that many people out of the mix and your receipts are naturally going to be down." George takes a slug of decaf, his eyes glued to the rising steam.

"That's certainly part of it, but
our problems in the morning
started before that. I'm talking
about our regulars who haven't
moved away. We're losing them;
and because the dot-coms *are*
moving, we have to work even
harder to keep our other customers."

"Look! If you're trying to tell me something, why
don't you just come out and say it? You think this
is my fault, don't you?"

"I didn't say that."

"You don't have to. I can read your expression.
You know, it's not easy having to deal with the
same things day after day. You're not here much
anymore, Jack. I think you've forgotten what a
challenge it is to always be on, to always have to
smile and be nice no matter how you feel. Or
what kind of day *you're* having."

"No, I know. It's not always as easy as we'd like it
to be."

"Can we finish this later? I need the men's room."
George turns and walks away, the last of his coffee sloshing in his cup.

Well. That certainly didn't go as well as I could have hoped for, Jack thinks. We didn't resolve anything. Maybe when my new consultant shows up, I'll ask her how she would have handled this.

MAKE IT PERSONAL
Everybody wants to be a regular

The voodoo priest and all his powders were as nothing compared to espresso, cappuccino, and mocha, which are stronger than all the religions of the world combined, and perhaps stronger than the human soul itself.
—Mark Helprin, *Memoir from Antproof Case*

The El Espresso
Pine Street and Fourth Avenue
Downtown Seattle
9:55 A.M.

The first wave of morning coffee-break customers has not quite started. Jack Hartman takes the opportunity to pull a latte and take it to a woman sitting on a bench across from the El. She's been sitting there since he arrived nearly ninety minutes ago, apparently waiting for someone to show up—someone who, as of this moment, is still officially missing.

"Here," Jack says as he hands her the latte, "I thought you might like this while you're waiting. He must be pretty special. What's his name?"

"Why, thank you for the coffee. His name is Jack and I'm beginning to think he is. Special, that is."

"His name is Jack? What a coincidence. So's mine."

"The Jack I'm supposed to meet is somewhat of an expert, I hear, on making lattes," she teases.

"And, do I have the honor of meeting Ms. Carol Wisdom?"

"You do."

"What are you doing sitting over here? I was expecting you to show up at the store at ten."

"Well, Jack, when I can, I like to observe my clients in action without them knowing I'm there. It sort of gives me an objective head start in learning who they are. I've actually been here—"

"For two days," Jack responds. "I know. I've been watching you."

Carol's initial shock at having been found out gives way to a gentle, appreciative laugh.

"I should have known I couldn't get much past you."

"Thanks, but tell me: what have you noticed so far? Do you have the answers I need to get the El back on track, so to speak?"

"It's been an interesting experience so far, Jack, I must say. And I've learned a lot, but not as much as I'm sure I'll learn now that we can finally talk with each other. And, yes, I'm certain we can get you back on track. I think you're going to be surprised by what I've discovered."

"As long as it's a good surprise. Where do we start?"

"Well, I always like to start by asking questions. Are you up for a morning interrogation or do you need to mind the store?"

"Yes, I'm ready—and no, I don't need to do a thing. George and Elizabeth have things under control for at least the next forty-five minutes or so."

"Was that George you were talking to? How'd your conversation go?"

Jack looks at Carol out of the corner of his eye. "It went OK. Not exactly the way I hoped it would, but I'll deal with it later. Now, what do you want to know?"

"Well, as I recall from the background info you sent, your customer count has fallen significantly, mostly due to the departure of a major corporation from a nearby office building. You're not sure you can make it without increasing your volume, and you're not sure what to do next. Is that a fair assessment of your problem?"

"Yeah. Throw in a few problems with employees and my own personal malaise and I think we're on target."

"You're on target in more ways than you think, Jack. I've been watching your customers for two days now and I've seen a great number of repeat visitors—people who are here two or three times a day, sometimes more."

"Yeah, we do have pretty loyal customers, I guess."

"You do. And that's directly connected to what I'm going to say next, which I'm sorry to say will probably sound a little like it came from a Management 101 lecture. But it helps to explain what's been happening to The El Espresso."

"A lecture, huh? Well, go ahead. I guess I can go back to school for a *few* minutes."

"Thanks. In my work, I deal with companies of all sizes, all around the world, and what we've been seeing recently is a definite and distinct loss of loyalty—both from customers and employees," Carol says. "You've heard the terms 'rightsizing, downsizing, and tightsizing'?"

Jack nods.

"Well, those were fancy words in the '70s, '80s, and '90s for companies' laying off their employees. As you can guess, one of the results was the loss of employee loyalty.

"Our grandparents and our par-ents were able to retire from the same company that gave them their first jobs. They could work thirty, forty, even fifty years with the same organi-zation and be assured of a weekly paycheck, a family of coworkers, and

a pension at retirement. And for the most part, they were fiercely loyal to the company that made all this possible.

"What the companies who did all the 'sizing' in the last few decades *didn't* count on was the direct connection between employee loyalty and customer loyalty. The companies were sure they were going to take some hits from their laid-off employees, but what they *hadn't* counted on was the translation in loss of loyalty from their employees to their customers. It turns out that customers are loyal when employees are loyal; when employee loyalty wanes, so does customer loyalty. When employees are loyal, they act selflessly. That is, they think about what's good for the company first, not about what's good for them. When employees *lose* their loyalty, it's hard for them to be selfless with the customers. As employees distance themselves from the company, they become antagonistic. Then they let that antagonism show in the way they act toward the customers and the way they talk about the company."

Jack nods again, looking thoughtful.

"Sorry about all that academic history, Jack, but what I've observed at The El Espresso over the last two days is more like the America of the 1950s than of the 2000s."

"That's good?"

"Oh, yes, Jack. That's great! I can tell from what I've seen, and what I've heard from your customers—"

"You've been talking to my customers?"

"Of course. I've talked to at least thirty of them since I've been here."

"I guess I'm not quite as observant as I thought," Jack says, a smile creeping across his face.

"Don't be too hard on yourself," Carol laughs. "You were busy running a business. Anyway, what I've observed is that loyalty to The El Espresso is probably the foremost trait of your customers. They not only love your coffee, they love *you*. They love you so much they've followed you every time you've changed locations. I'm pretty sure I know how you achieved that, but just to help you understand your company a little better, I'd like you to take a shot at telling *me* why you think your customers are so loyal. What in your opinion makes them willing to stand outside in line, in the rain sometimes, to get a cup of coffee that they could get at any of the chain coffee shops across the street and around the corner and sit inside where it's comfortable and dry?"

"It wasn't something I planned, Carol. They just do."

"I think it's more than that. Explain it to me the best you can."

"Well, ever since I was pouring coffee at thirty thousand feet, I've known that how I behaved affected how my passengers behaved. If I was having a bad day and I let them know it, I got back from them what I gave them. If I acted aloof, I got aloof back. If I was tired or annoyed at something that had happened earlier, suddenly my passengers were all grumpy too. Now I try not to distance myself from my customers. I try to make things personal."

"How do you mean?"

"For me, Carol, it's pretty simple. I treat my customers as friends first instead of customers. I always figure it's like the TV show *Cheers*—everybody wants to be a regular somewhere. Remember, the theme song said something about '. . . where everybody knows your name'? Well, one thing I've always done is learn my customers' names, and I drill it into my employees' heads as one of the most important things that differentiates us from the competition. It's surprising how much of a difference that makes, using their names."

"So, you make it personal by learning their names, but I'm sure you do more than that."

"Sure. I learn what they drink so they don't have to ask for it. They don't even have to say 'the usual.' We already know what it is and we have it ready for them by the time they get to the head of the line. But we also make it a point of learning something about them, like what they do for a living, what they like to do when they're not working, how many people in their family. Things like that."

"So you try to create a stronger connection between you and them through acquiring knowledge about them?"

"We don't think about it in those terms, but, yeah, I guess you're right."

"How *do* you strengthen the connection?"

"Lots of ways," Jack answers, "but because we like work to be fun, I try to do things to get the customers involved. Sometimes I even write down a question of the day on the chalkboard you see over there and ask customers to respond. Now, not everybody is what I like to call a 'Hokey Pokey Person,' so I respect the desire to get involved or not and I don't force this on everyone. But you'd be surprised how many people will take the invitation to talk seriously. You remember that Art Linkletter program, *Kids Say the Darndest Things*?

Well, around here we call it 'The El Espresso
Customers Say the Darndest Things.' Once people feel comfortable talking, they tell you stuff.
And when I see them again, I try to pick up on
the conversation we were having earlier or the day
before or whenever.

"What's surprising is that when you have this
personal relationship with your customers, the
day goes faster. When you serve your friends at
your house, you do special things for them, right?
Well, the same thing happens when your customers are friends. You find yourself thinking
about what they'd like and you treat them differently. And you know what? They treat you differently, too."

"And that makes them willing to
stand in line in the rain for a
cup of coffee?"

"Yes, I guess it does, because
they sure do it," Jack answers.
"I just remember when I was in college,
I worked for a theme park and all the college kids
used to talk about the customers as 'animals.'

They'd ask, 'How many animals in the corral, today?' Imagine—thinking of people as cattle! If my employees or I did that, I'm not sure I could get through the day—thinking about how many cups of coffee I'd have to pull before

I got to go home or what I had to do for the hundreds of 'animals' standing in line, all mooing and braying for things they wanted. What a zoo that would be!"

"Making It Personal is a great strategy, Jack. I wish more companies would think like that."

"I never actually thought of it as a strategy, Carol. It just seemed like the right thing to do. Once I saw individual people instead of cattle, once I greeted them by name, once I learned something about them, I started seeing them as friends, as family. And you know, I realized that I had begun to care about them, and that they had begun to care about me."

"How do you get your employees to make things personal?"

"I don't have a training class for it, or an instruction manual," Jack answers. "I guess it sort of happens. To start with, though, I hire people who have passion—passion about life, about coffee, about other people. Then I teach them how to pull coffee. I guess while they're hanging around me learning to pull a good cup, they just sort of pick up on making things personal."

"There's something else I see happening here, Jack. When you make things personal and you and your customers get to know more about each other, what you do is develop a community of customers, a group of people who are connected to each other in more ways than just the coffee, which is the core reason they're here. We know, for example, that the more connections that exist between customers and employees, the greater the bond, the greater the loyalty, and the greater the financial success of the organization. When there is a community to which customers belong, they are loyal to each other and to that community. And if a business is at the core of the community, as yours is, then that business reaps the rewards of the loyalty people feel to the community as a whole."

"Wow, if you say so! I didn't know we were creating a community. Again, I never thought about it like that, it just seemed like the right thing to do, so I did it. But, you know what? You're right about that community thing. We've even had a couple meet each other in line and wind up getting married. That's the kind of community this is. And you know that probably explains why people will walk four and five blocks, past ten or more chain-owned coffee shops, to get their coffee from us.  It's interesting, and I never thought about this in such a way before you talked about community, but remember back in '99 when the World Trade Organization met here and there were those riots in the streets? We had rioters and police officers and regular customers all together in line and the chaos seemed to flow around us and not bother us. It was almost like this was an officially recog-

nized oasis of sanity in the midst of all the chaos,
a community of reason in a world gone mad.
If I hadn't been here myself, I don't think I would
have believed it."

"Well, Jack, even though I wasn't here, I believe it.
When you make things personal between your
employees and your customers, everybody wins."

"Speaking of customers, what *did* they say
to you?"

"Most of them had nothing but praise and lots
of good stories."

"Most, but not all? What did they have to say?
Specifically?"

"I taped their conversations. Would you like to
hear a few?"

"As they used to say on TV when I was a kid,
'Roll 'em, Lester!'"

~ ~

Pine Street and Fourth Avenue
Downtown Seattle
10:45 A.M.

"As you listen to the tape, Jack, I want you to
identify common themes in what they're saying.
What we're looking for when we develop a plan
to improve a business are ideas that work, so we
can implement more of them. Then we want to
identify the things that didn't work as well so we
can modify them. I think you know the first customer on this tape, a woman named Sally Norton."

"Sally's a nonfat cappuccino. She's the one I was
telling you about! The one who got married."

"I know. Listen."

Carol fast-forwards the cassette to a counter
number she reads off a clipboard and hits play.
The voice of Sally Norton, a Seattle bank executive, can be heard, the sounds of Seattle's downtown evident behind her.

"I became an El customer in '82. I had tasted
some of the awful instant 'international' coffees

my mom used to stir up and, frankly, I couldn't understand how people could drink the stuff. One of my colleagues at the bank brought me a cappuccino from the El one day and I was hooked. I've been a regular customer for twenty years. I've followed them through six locations. But the most important thing the El ever did for me was find me a husband."

Carol says off-mike: "Find you a husband?"

"Yup," Sally continues. "For several weeks back in May of '92, I kept noticing this really attractive man who'd buy a ristretto every day about the same time as I got my nonfat cappuccino. Eventually, it sort of worked out that we would be standing next to each other in line. We started talking, he asked me out, and pretty soon we were dating. To make a long story short, we got married and Dave and I always celebrate our anniversary here with Jack and the gang. I sometimes don't know where I'd be if it weren't for the El. As long as they're in business, they've got me as a customer."

Carol stops the tape, checks her clipboard, and hits fast forward.

"Sounds like you've got a customer for life, Jack."

"Every time Sally meets someone new in line, she tells that story. I like to kid her that she's given more performances of that than *A Chorus Line*."

"The next one is David Nedleman, a securities lawyer."

"Vanilla latte," Jack responds immediately.

"I live two blocks from here," the radio-announcer-quality baritone says from Carol's tape. "The El's my neighbor. We're having a condo association meeting tonight and I've got to bring some of Jack's chocolate chip cookies. If I show up without them, I never hear the end of it. When I have to be at the court-house, I sometimes stop at one of the chain places and I have to check my drink every time because they get it wrong so often. That never happens

here. Not only do they know what I drink but by
the time I get to the front of the line, it's ready
and all I have to do is pay for it. I like to deal
with a business where they're serious about what
they do."

Carol, off-mike again: "Most people use the
word 'playful' when they talk about the El but
you used the term 'serious.' What do you mean
by that?"

"By serious, I mean attention to detail. That's the
essence of professionalism. In my line of work,
I have to be professional all the time so I've come
to expect it as a matter of course. Don't get me
wrong, these guys have fun here. If they didn't,
it would be like any other coffee joint. So I guess
what I'm really saying is that they're serious about
having fun at what they do. And what they do is
get things right."

"You know," Jack says while Carol is readying the
next cut she intends to play, "Dave was talking
about having his drink ready. We try to anticipate
and do that for everyone. But I have to admit,
Carol, I worry about being presumptuous—what

if someone wants something different that day and I've already made their usual?"

"OK, answer your own question, Jack. If that happened, what would you do?"

"I'd make them what they wanted and give theirs to someone walking by, maybe one of the homeless we have around here."

"I thought as much," Carol says. "I think you'll recognize this next voice as Mary Sue Springer's."

"Tall nonfat mocha. Mary Sue is one of the best real estate agents in town."

"This is always my first stop of the day," Mary Sue says, "and it pretty much sets the tone for the rest of it. I live in the suburbs so on the weekends I have to get my coffee at one of the chains. I just find them so impersonal these days and they often get my order wrong. It's like the kids they have working there don't really listen to what you're saying. Anyway, they act like they'd just as soon be done for the day and it's only nine in the morning. When I come to the El, they always

know what I want and they really care about what they're doing. My mocha is always exactly the way I like it. I wish Jack would open a store in my neighborhood."

"Sorry. I tried that once. Never again," Jack says over Mary Sue, who is now talking about loyalty and passion.

"What seems to happen is that a company starts out with a good product and they become success-ful with it and then they start to focus on profits instead of the product and the service. Thank goodness that hasn't happened here. Everything's as good as it always was. Personally, I attribute that to Jack's passion for coffee. I know I have to be passionate about selling real estate and honoring people's lifestyles or I won't succeed. I see the same thing here. Make no mistake about it, the El's coffee is the best. But if they weren't passion-ate about keeping it that way and about keeping their cus-tomers happy—keeping *me* happy—I'd be long gone. Life's too short to

spend money with companies that don't care about you."

Carol's voice on tape can be heard asking, "How much of your loyalty is to Jack and how much is it to the El? In other words, do you think Jack's passion has trickled down through the entire operation?"

"I'm loyal to both. Of course, the majority of the passion comes from Jack, but also from his wife, Dianne, when she was here. But the passion I see now is steeped all through the company. You can also see it in the devotion all the baristas have for the customers. To them, the customers come first and service is king. I just feel at home here."

"Next we have Melissa Crosby," Carol says to Jack.

"Regular latte and a hot cocoa for her daughter, Katie."

"For me, the reason I come here is that everything is just the way I like it," Melissa says. "The latte is

perfect, and I know the names of everyone behind
the counter. I even know the names of many
of the people who wait in line with me. I like the
fact that they know my name and what I drink.
It makes me feel like I belong. If I don't start out
my day at the El, my routine is shot and the whole
day is ruined."

"I don't know if she told you or not," Jack says,
"but Melissa imports Chinese antiques and she and
her family spent several years in Hong Kong. She
says that the taste for fine coffee that started here
in Seattle has now spread around the world. And
she claims that it all began at The El Espresso."

"How does that make you feel?" Carol asks.

"Well, if it's true, I'm a little awed."

"And if it isn't?" Carol asks, carefully.

"Well, then, we'll just have to work a little
harder.

"To be honest, there *are* some areas your customers feel could use a little of that hard work.

Fortunately, for you, this next interview is not representative of the majority of your customers, but it does point up some the problems you're already aware of. This is David Green."

"Sorry. Don't know him."

Carol hit play and settled back to watch Jack's reactions.

"I like the coffee a lot. It's why I come back, even if the service is a little inconsistent."

Carol's voice can be heard off mike, "And how long have you been coming here?"

"I just started as a security guard in that building over there about, what? Four months ago? I mostly come in the mornings. You never know how long the line's going to be. And sometimes the person who makes my coffee seems to be somewhere else. Sometimes, they screw up my order."

Carol's voice can be heard again, "But you keep coming back?"

"Yeah, it's convenient and the coffee's good. But there's a new place gonna open up a block the other direction from my job and when it does, I'll give it a try. I like the coffee here but it's not the only place around."

Carol hits the stop button and begins to put away her clipboard and disconnect the recorder. "I have to say there were several other people who mentioned inconsistent service in the mornings, too."

Jack sighs. "I guess I already knew that."

Carol looks at the El and then back at Jack. "Keep in mind that when you listen to feedback the most important thing to do is hear those things you've done well and make plans to continue doing them. Then you make note of those things you haven't done so well and make plans to do them better. If you only focus on the negative, you're doing yourself and your employees a total disservice."

Jack rubs imaginary dust from his knees and stands up. "Well, that's food for thought all right. So. Now that we're done with the feedback, can I buy you a double latte?"

Carol smiles. "I'd like that, Jack. I'd like that a lot."

PRODUCT
People don't pay good money for bad coffee

The use of coffee will probably become greatly extended—as in other countries, it may diffuse itself among the mass of the people and make a considerable ingredient in their daily sustenance.
—Benjamin Moseley, 1785

The El Espresso
Pine Street and Fourth Avenue
Downtown Seattle
Noon

"Know what I'd like to talk about now?" Carol Wisdom asks, the remains of the steaming double latte in her hands.

"What?" Jack says.

"The coffee. The product you sell."

"You've come to the right place, then. They say some people don't know beans, but I do. I can talk beans for hours, if you'd like."

"I think I can listen as long as you can talk," Carol says. "If you don't mind, I'm going to record this for my notes."

"I don't mind at all. Let's see. Beans. Where do I start?"

"How about this? Are you using the same kind of beans today as when you started?"

"Good question. I don't think anyone has ever asked me that before but the answer is no. When Dianne and I bought The El Espresso, we bought the whole shebang—cart, cups, vendors, procedures, everything. As we began to learn how the business worked and understand the nuances, we got to be confident enough to make changes. Not change for the sake of change, mind you, but changes we felt were going to improve the product mix and ultimately improve the business. So the first thing I did was research beans themselves. I read everything I could and then had our vendor sell us different kinds of beans. And we experimented. We had them roasted longer, at different temperatures, and we ground them different ways, at different levels of coarseness. We experimented on just ourselves at first, then with friends who knew good coffee, then with some of our better customers. Then we introduced a new drink so we could get the new beans into the mix, so to speak. That way, we didn't need to make a drastic, untested change—not like Coke did when they tried to replace classic Coke with New Coke."

"I remember. Coca-Cola was trying to outsell Pepsi by changing their product so that it tasted more like Pepsi, which is what their research on younger Americans showed them was the way to go."

"Yeah, but they forgot to ask you and me what we preferred. I don't think they even make New Coke anymore at all. Anyway, Dianne and I didn't want anything like that to happen at the El. So we found ways to make changes and introduce new products that were less flamboyant and had a chance to generate a following and create word-of-mouth advertising. That's how our burnt-creme latte was born. Today it's one of the drinks for which we're known," Jack says with a touch of pride.

"Were you successful at finding better beans?"

"From the way we've managed to increase our sales and maintain our customer base, I'd say we were. Not that it was easy, mind you. It took a while for us to find the best beans for each drink and learn to roast and grind them the right way. But that wasn't all we had to get right. We had to learn to pull the perfect cup. That means the right amount of grounds with the right amount of water at the right temperature to yield the most aromatic and flavorful coffee. At the same time we decided that a perfect cup at the El would always be made with a double shot. That way our coffee would always be twice as good as the competition's.

"What's interesting to me is that the hardest part wasn't finding the *right* ways to do these things."

"It wasn't?" Carol says, obviously surprised. "What was?"

"Maintaining. Being consistent. So that no matter when you come to The El Espresso and no matter whether I'm here making your coffee, or it's Elizabeth instead, you'll get exactly the drink you expect. Exactly the drink you remember. Exactly the experience that makes you want to come back—cup after cup, day after day, year after year."

"So, if I'm hearing you correctly, having the right product is a combination of the right beans, knowing how to prepare them the right way, and

training your employees to pull
each drink the same way each
and every time they make it."

"Not only that," the El's owner
quickly adds. "You have to have
the right kind of employees, the
right ambiance, the right pricing,
the right product mix, the right kind
of customers, and the right location."

"Or, in your case, the right locations, *plural*. You've
moved, what, six times? And your customers have
followed you each time. Right product? Or right
service? Or right employees?"

"Right. All of that. I'm sure you know that bad
product overrides good service, that a poor product will drive away good customers. And not even
superlative service can overcome bad product.
If you don't have a good cup of coffee, they won't
pay you good money for it."

"The reverse is true, you know. Bad service can
drive customers away from a good product."

"Absolutely right," Jack says, "There's no question that our success is a result of a blend of several things. I know for certain that if we didn't serve a great cup of coffee—what some people even call the best in Seattle—we'd have been out of business four moves ago. With all the fine coffee shops in town, we'd have lost our people to them the minute we tried to sell a poorly pulled cup of coffee. That's why I make sure we have standards and that everyone keeps them. When the wholesale price of our beans goes up, for example, I won't change to cheaper beans just to keep the retail price of a cup the same. I'll either take the hit myself or, if it's a very severe price increase, pass it along to the customers. But, of course, we'll put up all kinds of signs explaining the price increases. But, you know what? The customers don't mind if the price goes up as long as the quality remains consistent—and I tell them *why* the price went up!"

"What you've been talking about is exactly the kind of thing I tell all my clients," Carol says.

"You tell them how to buy coffee beans?"

"No, Jack. What I meant was I tell them if they want to be successful in business, the first thing is they have to get the fundamentals right. In your case, the fundamentals start with the product, the coffee. When you started the El you had a passion for coffee. Today, you still have that passion for the coffee but it now encompasses the passion for pulling it perfectly."

"I hadn't really thought about it in those terms, but you're right."

"Your clients—your customers—have remained loyal because you have never compromised on quality," Carol continues. "More than that, you've done it in the spirit of fun, which in turn has created community. And community creates and maintains loyalty. So you see, the relationship your customers have with The El Espresso enhances their feeling about the quality of your product. It's a reinforcing cycle: as long as they love coming here, and as long as the product maintains its high standards, their feelings for the El keep growing—they begin to take on mythic proportions. In their minds, there is simply no other coffee like yours. But let the product quality slip and suddenly things are not as much fun and your customer base begins to experiment with buying coffee from other places in search of the mythic cup of coffee they feel they can no longer get here."

"That's so true. Dianne and I have had several favorite restaurants that we no longer go to because they changed something—the chef, the place they bought their ingredients, something—and the food just didn't taste the same anymore. It wasn't as good. Eventually we just stopped going there. Sometimes it wasn't even a conscious decision, we just stopped going," Jack says, a little lost in his personal recollections.

"That's how it is when quality is allowed to slip—companies lose business. For years, Ford's television commercials have used the tagline 'Quality Is Job One' to underscore their unique marketing concept. The reality is that's how we *all* should think about quality. It's job one. In today's new work environments, no longer is quality control the responsibility of one person or one department. It's no longer the responsibility of the Director of Product Quality—it's everybody's. Studies show that the most successful businesses are those in which the employees take ownership, account-ability, and responsibility not only for their actions but for the quality and consistency of the product itself."

"It *is* all about the product, isn't it?" Jack says.

Carol sits back. "Yes and no. There isn't much in life that can exist independently and it seems that the most successful concepts, people, and busi-nesses are interdependent—somehow connected so that a change in one area creates a change in the others. In the case of product, there's an inter-esting correlation between quality and employee loyalty, and you know from our past conversation how that translates into customer loyalty as well. Studies have shown that as the quality of the prod-uct rises, so does employee loyalty. Employees who are proud of the product they make, or the service they provide, enjoy coming to work. They anticipate the new day. And as we all know, when we are enthusiastic about what we are doing, we do better work. And better work creates higher-quality results. So the cycle looks like this: high product quality generates high employee loyalty, which translates to high enthusiasm, which generates higher-quality work, which translates to higher product quality."

"More Management 101?" Jack says, smiling.

"Yup," Carol says, smiling back. "And here's the payoff. The message for business owners is: Be passionate about your quality, celebrate that quality in word and deed, and your people will be passionate about their work. For employees the message is: Be proud about your work and what you produce and you will make your work environment more enjoyable."

"Wow! All this from a simple cup of coffee. Who'da thunk it?" Jack says, tongue in cheek.

"Who, indeed?" Carol replies, draining the last bit of foam from her latte.

THE EYE OF INTENTION

If you don't know where you're going, you won't know when you get there

Coffee: black as hell, strong as death, sweet as love.
—Turkish proverb

The El Espresso
Pine Street and Fourth Avenue
1:30 P.M.

The lunch hour rush is over. Jack is helping
George and Elizabeth straighten up as he and

Carol await the arrival of Jack's wife. Ostensibly, Dianne is stopping by with supplies for The El Espresso. In point of fact, she has arranged her visit to make sure that Carol Wisdom hears all sides of the story.

Dianne is leery about hiring a business consultant because she figures the consultant will recommend expanding their operation to more locations in an effort to improve revenues and cash flow. When Dianne arrives with a handtruck full of boxes, concern is clearly visible on her face, a fact that Carol addresses even before Dianne has a chance to speak.

"Hi, Dianne. I'm Carol Wisdom. Jack's going to take care of the supplies so you and I can talk without interruption."

"Oh, good. Thanks, Jack. Let me pull a couple of lattes and we can talk. I've been looking forward to this all day."

"Actually, I'm going to switch to cocoa if you don't mind," Carol says. "I hear it's fantastic too."

"Oh, that's right. You're not from Coffeetown USA. You're not used to all the caffeine we consume," Dianne laughs.

After the drinks are made, the two women make their way to one of the concrete benches—where Seattle's downtown bicycle messengers hold each day's morning meetings—and begin their conversation.

"I understand from some of the things that Jack has alluded to that you're a little apprehensive about my being here. Is there anything I can do to make you feel more comfortable about our work together? I know you've played a major role in this business and your input is vital."

"Thank you, Carol. I guess apprehensive is a good word. I just wasn't sure what your suggestions to us might be."

"Just as long as it doesn't include expansion, right?"

Dianne says, relief sliding across her face, "So you know?"

"I know that in '91 you tried expansion with less-than-favorable results. Why don't you fill me in on the details?"

"OK. I don't know how well you remember 1991 but the country was dealing with a small-scale recession, even though you couldn't tell it by our sales, which were actually up substantially over 1990. Starbucks had made the leap from one  store that roasted and sold coffee beans in the Public Market to a series of small stores that sold coffee to go. We'd been in business more than ten years and our customers were afraid that this new competition from Starbucks would put us out of business. Actually, I think it helped us."

"How's that?" Carol asks, sipping her cocoa.

"With more locations serving high-quality coffee with a high-ticket price, people got used to the idea of paying more for quality coffee. And our quality was high enough that we didn't lose anybody to the competition. In fact, I think we picked up customers from them."

"And why was that?"

"Well, quite frankly, I believe our coffee is the best you can get, we have better people, and the whole atmosphere is just nicer at the El. You know?"

"Believe me, I know."

"Well, anyway, we were doing pretty well," Dianne says. "Keep in mind we operated from a cart at the entrance to the Monorail, and people had become used to getting their coffee from us on their way to work. We were getting noticed by all sorts of folks and were winning awards from magazines and television. We were always at the top of the newspaper readers' polls for 'Best Coffee in Seattle.' We had a lot of people coming to us to try our coffee and there was plenty of room for everybody in those days. Still is, as a matter of fact."

"Sounds like everything was working according to plan."

"Well, that was kind of the problem. We didn't *have* a plan. We were just going along, day to day, making enough to meet our needs and put a little away. We did enough to buy our place on Bainbridge, so I guess we were actually doing pretty well. And when a longtime customer came to us with a plan to expand, we were flattered. But because we didn't have a clear vision of our business we didn't know how to evaluate our options appropriately."

"And so, you did what?"

"We expanded. See, this customer had lived in Europe for many years and really knew great coffee. She constantly told us ours was the best she'd ever tasted. Over the course of a few months, she con-  vinced us that the only way we could stay in business in the face of the rapid Starbucks expansion was for us to expand, too. Because our coffee was far superior, she said, we would take customers from them anytime our shops went head-to-head. We actually had a little experience by that time running successful multiple operations because we had started the original espresso stand at Nordstrom's during the Christmas holidays. We'd probably still be running that location to this day if they hadn't seen how much business we were doing and decided to run it themselves. Anyway, when she created this business plan that called for dozens of locations, we were sure we could handle it without compromising the values of the business or the quality of the product. Besides, isn't that what you're *supposed* to do when you become successful? Grow? Expand?"

"That does seem to be what people think," Carol agrees. "How'd you do with it?"

"Well, we started with two additional carts outside the downtown area. We made money, but we hated it! In fact, Jack thinks of the whole experience as a failure."

"I wouldn't exactly call it a failure," Jack says, sitting down next to Dianne, the supplies all stowed away in their tiny space, "but it's certainly not something I would want to deal with again. It was a tough time. Dianne ran our main location and I spent my time growing the new business. I was always hiring and training new employees, surveying new business locations, juggling loan payments, and trying to make sure that the coffee stayed worth drinking while the business was growing."

"Jack hated being a manager," Dianne adds. "He missed seeing his everyday customers, he hated the time lost traveling between locations, and he spent so much of his day training employees that he felt like he was no longer in the business of serving coffee to friends. He was in the business of business building. He truly hated the whole thing."

"So what happened?" Carol asks Jack.

"Eventually we sold the carts to individuals who just wanted to have their own businesses then we put our tails between our legs and retrenched to operating our one cart at one location. Maybe we weren't as successful as we could have been, but I have to tell you we're a darn sight happier today."

"That is not at all an uncommon story, guys,"
Carol says. "Don't look so downcast. You weren't
defeated. Your problems were not ones of failure
versus success, your problems were ones of intention versus opportunity. And you tried to do it
all without a plan."

"Our partner *did* have a *business* plan," Dianne
says, a touch of defensiveness in her voice.

"That's not the kind of plan I'm talking about.
I mean a strategic plan. For the two of you, for
the El itself. See, if you don't know where you're
going in business or in life, or what you intend to
have happen along the way, you can't effectively
decide what to do next or if you're even *on* the
road to success. Without a plan, it's not possible
to accurately determine what success is. You can
only judge your results by looking at them based
on your intentions."

"You know," Jack says, a gleam of understanding
in his eyes, "when we were expanding, some people thought *that* was success."

"But not for you, right?"

"Right! Not for me. I hated it. To me, *not* spending time pulling great coffee and talking to my customers felt like failure."

"That's the key," Carol explains. "Before you can become successful in your work, you have to define for yourself what success means to you. Each of us may define success differently, yet we often use the same yardstick to measure it. That's not fair. In your case, success meant creating a business that would allow you to continue to do every day those elements of your airline stewing career that were the most rewarding. Namely, making great coffee and turning passengers, or customers, into friends."

"And, of course," Dianne adds, "making enough money to stay alive and enjoy life."

"Of course. Many of the most successful people have come to realize that if they aren't lucky enough to be earning a living doing what they enjoy most, they'd better learn to love what they *are* doing so they can earn enough to do what they really enjoy. It's like the Crosby, Stills, and Nash song that goes, "If you can't be with the one you love, love the one you're with."

"You know," Jack says, his eyes staring at the growing line of people waiting to get their afternoon lattes from the El, "I've been thinking about expanding the business."

"What!?" Dianne says, nearly falling off the bench.

"Calm down, Dianne. That's not what I meant. I meant that I've been thinking about the *need* people in business seem to have to expand. And I think I've learned something—at least about me."

Dianne sighs and gives him the look that means, "OK, tell me." Jack sees it and continues.

"When you're successful at what you've been doing, and there's no doubt that we were extremely successful, you want to share that success with more and more people. It seems an easy thing to do. And, of course, there's that anticipation of increasing your income with what appears to be minimal effort. So people in business look to grow their companies through expansion— bigger stores, more of them. For me, that was not a viable option. What happened is that I was spending too much time working *on* the business rather than *in* it."

"Which is exactly the kind of behavior you want to encourage if you're *trying* to grow a business," Carol adds. "Spend more time *on* the business than *in* it."

"Exactly," Jack says. "But I love the hands-on, the day-to-day, too much. I can't give it up. I like working *in* the business. And while I have the entrepreneurial spirit that enjoys starting and running my own business, I am *not* an entrepreneur."

"You're not?" Dianne asks.

"No, he's not," Carol says. "I was hoping you would understand that, Jack."

"If Jack Hartman, the man who turned latte into a household word in America, isn't an entrepreneur," Dianne questions, "what in the world is he?"

"I'm a small business owner," Jack responds immediately. "It's not the same thing at all. I love what I do and I do it well. But I don't want to grow and I don't want to *build* a business. I don't have any idea about starting something else—now or ever. Entrepreneurs love the start-up phase and the confusion and challenge that comes with that. What I love is working with people on maintaining the business. Think about this, Dianne. I'm doing *my* expanding—the sharing of our success—by helping other people start and run their own coffee businesses. That's my version of expanding."

"Yeah," Dianne says, "when David wanted to go out on his own, you helped him get started. Maria followed her passion for coffee to Europe and you gave her all sorts of advice. And whenever someone else starts a business up and down the street, even competitors, Jack is always the first one there offering his support and suggestions—if they're interested. That does make sense."

"I think there's room for both big *and* small companies to survive in the coffee business in this town," Jack says. "In fact, I think there's room for big and small companies in *any* business in *any* town—if each of them goes about it in the right way and stays true to its own intentions."

"You're right about the size thing, Jack," Carol says. "Remember a few years ago when Rally's Hamburgers started up? They decided that what McDonald's, Burger King, and Wendy's had forgotten was their origins—hamburgers for people literally on the run. So they built small drive-through stores next to their bigger competitors and offered inexpensive hamburgers, cheese-burgers, shakes, and spicy fries. And look at them today—a small business that's successful operating in the shadow of the country's fast-food giants."

"Even *that's* too big for me," Jack says. "I only want one store. But I'll help anyone else who wants to have one too. That's my version of expansion—keep it simple. Let everybody have a piece of the action. Work enough to make money but leave enough time to do the other things you enjoy. Love what you do and do what you love. Understand what makes you happy and do it. To me, those are the secrets of being successful at work, whether you own the business or are one of the people who make the business go."

"I don't know if it's the caffeine I've consumed in the last few days or talking to you guys or listening to your customers," Carol says, an introspective gleam in her eyes, "but I'm beginning to see a pattern here. Give me a few minutes, and another latte, and let me see if I can synthesize what I've learned."

"Great, I'll pull," Jack says, leaping up from his spot on the bench.

"No, you big lug," Dianne says in her mock-1940s movie accent, "it's my turn to pull."

"Whatever you say, kiddo. Whatever you say."

THE FOUR P'S
Big lessons from a small cup of coffee

O Coffee, thou dost dispel all care;
thou art the object of desire to the scholar.
—Arabic Poem

The El Espresso
Pine Street and Fourth Avenue
Downtown Seattle
3:00 P.M.

Jack and Dianne Hartman are busy straightening things that don't need straightening and helping employees Anne Martin and Deirdre O'Neill pull coffee for the never-ending line of customers. Carol, yet another latte at her side, sits on the bench consulting her notes, listening to her tape recordings of El customers and employees, and entering thoughts into her laptop. From the smiles of recognition on her face and periodic nods of her head, it's apparent she's pleased with the results of her three days of fieldwork at the El. Finally, Carol closes her computer and beckons Jack and Dianne to join her.

Carol begins. "So, if you remember, my first question about The El Espresso was 'Why are customers willing to stand in line rain or shine to get their coffee?' Well, after talking to you two today and your customers yesterday, I think I finally have the answers."

"And will these answers help us replace the customers we've lost?" Jack wants to know.

"I think they will," Carol answers as she begins to lay out what she's discovered about how and why The El Espresso has been so successful.

"Let me start by saying that The El Espresso has been successful due to both of you and your hard work, intuition, and passion. The things you've done and the reasons behind them are responsible for the reputation and standing you have in the community."

"That's great," Jack says, "Only how come we don't know what those things are? If they're our ideas, why aren't they obvious to us?"

"When you live something as intensely as the two of you have, it isn't always easy to stand back and see what you're doing. As a consultant, I have the advantage and opportunity to observe your work, to ask you questions, and to bring an unbiased point of view to the situation. Just because you may not be able to express these principles at the moment doesn't mean they aren't true, or that you don't unconsciously use them on a daily basis, or that they aren't at work even while we are speaking. That's the thing about universal principles—they work whether you believe in them or not."

Jack and Dianne sit on either side like bookends and listen as Carol Wisdom continues.

"To see what you need to do to overcome what you've lost since that big dot-com moved out, you need to know what  you did to get the business in the first place. Often the secret to success in bad times is to do what you did when you created the good times to begin with. To figure that out for a client, the first thing I do is look at what's changed besides the apparent immediate cause of the downturn.

"Since you started more than twenty years ago, you've moved locations several times. For most retailers, especially ones like the El that rely on convenience of location to directly drive customer traffic, that alone could kill the business. But it didn't. In fact, each time you moved, not only did your established customers follow you but you generated new customers at the new location as well. So I've ruled out location as a problem.

"Another potential problem is employees. Since you started you've had nearly four dozen of them. As in most service organizations, your employees are the direct link to your customers. Not only bad employees can hurt you, the good ones can too."

"How can good employees hurt you?" Dianne asks.

"When a service business relies on its employees to be everything to the customer—say, a restaurant built around a famous chef—and that icon for the business leaves, relocates, or starts a competing business, the original company can lose customers—if not its very existence—to that employee. In your case, not only have good employees left and started competing firms but you've actually helped them—and still your business maintained the loyalty of its customer base. So it wasn't changing employees either.

"Next, I've looked at what hasn't changed. And while there are many things that for the most part haven't changed over the years, I've distilled the main elements into five areas: Passion, People, Personal, Product, and Intention."

"Maybe we should call them 'The Four P's,'"
Dianne says, half jokingly. "Oh, and I know! 'The
Eye of Intention.'"

"I like that, Dianne," Carol says. "Maybe they'll
be easier to remember that way. So the first 'P'
would be Passion. You both have it. You have
passion for coffee, passion for the business, and
a passion for making people happy. If you didn't
have it, it would have been hard, if not impossi-
ble, to maintain the consistency you've managed
to achieve—even during the recent hard times
you've been going through."

Jack sat silently, considering her comment.

"When people do what they love, they feel like
what they do for a living isn't really work—
it's fun. When you listen to your heart, you discover your personal source of positive energy.
That's what you did when you bought the El.
The result was that you began to build your work
around your passion. And your vision for the
business—your intention—was a direct result of
your passion. You knew you wanted to pull the
perfect cup of coffee and teach people to love it

as much as you did. What you were actually doing was sharing your passion, passing it on to your customers and your employees. You were building a climate in which you, your customers, and your staff could express and share your passions—first about coffee and then about yourselves and the world around you. When you allow your passion to be the center of your work, your work becomes play. And that makes work fun, and ultimately successful."

"I have some questions on this," Jack says, "but let's go on. What's the next 'P'?"

"The second 'P' is for People: both your customers and your employees. As The El Espresso became successful, you surrounded yourself with good customers and good employees. Finding and creating good employees was your first chal-  lenge, and you met it and con- tinue to meet it every day. You look for people who share your values and then you train them in the skills they need to pull a good cup of coffee. As I recall,

you weren't interested in finding employees who'd worked for
another coffee company first,
you were looking for good
people who wanted to work
for you."

"That's right," Jack recalls. "In fact, quite a number of our staff were customers first. They loved
our coffee, what we stood for, and decided they
wanted to work in the business with us."

"That's exactly the point, Jack. Good people
become good employees. And when a company is
filled with good employees, guess what you get?"

"Good customers," Jack and Dianne say in
unison.

"You got it. Of course, the successful training and
developing of good employees is a direct result of
having passion. Passion is the fuel; employees are
the engines. When employees like what they're
doing, they become loyal. Loyal employees produce better product and service. Better product
and service attract better customers. And better

customers are loyal and ultimately mean greater lifetime value to a business.

"The way you keep your employees happy, Jack, is you create shared expectations *with* them and communicate your intentions *to* them. So, at any moment, they know what you expect *from* them. You don't use fear or force to get the results you want. What I see you do is honor all the individuals and value their contribution. That allows them to bring their best selves to work each day. And you encourage them to be successful—even if they want to leave and start a competing business!"

"OK . . . ," Jack admits. "What's the third 'P'?"

"It's the 'P' for Personal. You have to make it personal. By that I mean create a connection between the customer and the business that extends beyond the product, a connection that builds loyalty. In your case, you make your customers feel like this is their own personal coffee shop. Each of them feels like a regular. Whether you planned it this way or not, you've taken the time and energy to learn their names and what they drink. Not only does this speed up the transaction time for you, it lets them get on with their lives faster. And it gives them a feeling of community at the same time. To your customers, the El is the place where they come and everyone knows their name. When they come here, they are somebody, they feel like you care about them. And they know personal things about you, too: what you do, what you like, that you're happily married to each other. There is a mutual sharing of personal information that occurs during the standard course of commerce. All things being equal, we all want shopping experiences in which we are made to feel like friends instead of simply sources of revenue for the company. When you make it personal for the customer, you create exactly that kind of experi-ence—the kind they tell their friends, family, and coworkers about. For your customers, the El has become part of their lives. For them, their relationship to you is personal."

"I really hadn't thought of it quite like that," Dianne says, carefully considering the consultant's observations. "That's kind of an awesome responsibility."

"It can be," Carol responds, "but when you keep things fun, as you do, the relationship is enjoyable and profitable—for both sides!"

Carol consults her laptop and continues.

"The final 'P' is for Product—in your case, coffee. Product is the foundation of a business, for better or worse. Good product can sometimes make customers overlook lack of attention to the other three P's in a business, but the other P's may not be able to overcome the drastic and almost-always-fatal effects of bad product.

"Your success, Jack, is due in part to the fact that you are as passionate about your product as you are about your people. You told me you wouldn't sacrifice the quality of your beans for a lower price. So, as you built the business, you sought out the best beans, the best vendors. You developed the best ways to brew and serve your product. You asked your customers for their input and you respected it. That's because you know

instinctively that your product is not merely the
latte they walk away with but also the quality of
the experience itself. Combined, the coffee and
experience of purchasing it are the product for
which the El has become known.

"And you've delivered your product with consistency over time, through employee changes and
multiple changes of location. That consistency
of product creates customer confidence that
supports their desire to remain loyal. You and
Dianne, and all your employees, have earned a
well-deserved reputation for having a product
that customers love to talk about.

"Intention. Or, as you called it, the Eye of Intention. If you don't know clearly what you intend to
accomplish, there's simply no way to be effective.
Every result you achieve can only be evaluated
with regard to your intention. When your results
match your intentions, you have arrived at the
train-stop known as success."

Carol stopped, letting her words sink in. "And
that, in short, is why your customers are willing

to stand in line in the rain just to give you lots of money for a cup of coffee."

"Let me see if I have this," Jack says. "To make the El successful *again* we have to have passion, hire good people, create good customers, make the buying experience personal. Is that right, and maintain a good product?"

"That's it."

"Surely there's got to be more to running a good business than that. This Four P's stuff seems pretty simplistic."

"Clearly, there are fine points to being in business," Carol elaborates. "There are accounting principles, human resource procedures, and all sorts of fancy names for things, none of which can be ignored. But the truth of the matter is that the Four P's cover all the essential ingredients for success. If you get these fundamentals right, the rest will take of itself. If doing the books isn't your cup of coffee, hire an accountant."

"We already do that," Dianne admits.

"I like to think that life is made up of simple truths," Carol says. "And that whether or not you believe in them, they work—with or without you. Simple truths are like common sense. And while they may be common sense, they are not common practice. But they were for you when you started, and they're still common practice for you today."

"So, are you saying that to improve my customer base all we have to do is follow the Four P's?" Jack says, uncertainty evident in his voice.

"It may sound simple, but universal truths often do. Even though I came across the Four P's right here studying your business, these principles apply to any business, regardless of size or product. The Four P's are at work right now in thousands of companies, whether they know it or not."

"Even a company with hundreds of employees?"

"Have you ever heard of Jet Blue?"

"They're a new airline that flies from here to New York, right?" Dianne asks.

"That's them. Well, I've been following Jet Blue since they started up—in fact, I fly them every time I come out here—and I can tell you with complete certainty that the Four P's are part of their everyday philosophy."

"They call them the Four P's?"

"No. Because they're universal truths, it doesn't matter what they call them, they still work."

"How can you tell?" Jack asks.

"Let's go through them. Passion. David Neeleman, the founder, is passionate about creating an efficient, low-cost airline that treats people right. People. He hires the best, offers profit-sharing and stock options, and insists that any employees

who don't treat all their customers with respect
will be fired. Product. He's bought only one kind
of plane to reduce expenses, put leather seats
and satellite television in all of them, and given
free round-trip tickets to every passenger who had trouble with a flight.

Once, when a flight had to
be changed by two hours, he
helped call every scheduled
passenger to tell them of the
change.

"Personal. This is where he really shines. Once a
week he loads baggage, once a week he flies on his
airline, and when he does he meets and greets
each and every customer, thanking them for their
business."

"What about Intention?" Dianne asks.

"Simple. Neeleman plans to be one of only a
few airlines who make money and who are growing every year. And Jet Blue is just one example of
thousands of larger companies that employ the
Four P's and the Eye of Intention successfully."

"Do the Four P's and the Eye of Intention work for employees as well as owners?" Jack asks.

"Yes," Carol says, "it doesn't matter if you own the business, work in it, or are a manager. The Four P's and the Eye of Intention apply to you, your department, the entire company. If you have passion for what you do, hire the best people and be the best person you can be, make your working relationships personal, and maintain the highest quality for your product, you will be successful and so will the company. And along the way, you'll be able to bring your best self to your work. And that will make it an enjoyable experience— for yourself and the customers as well. Since you and I spend more of our life working than at any other single thing we do, we should make it as enjoyable as we can. Fortunately, enjoying our work has a beneficial side effect—it's profitable! And if you're not happy doing what you're doing, ask yourself why. And, more important, ask yourself what you can do to make work fun.

"The key is to know what your intentions are. Success can only be defined in terms of your intentions. Once you know what you want to achieve, then you can generate the plans to make it happen."

Carol looks at Dianne, who seems energized—then at Jack, who's slumped on the bench. "Jack, what is it that's bothering you?"

"I don't know, Carol. This Four P's and Eye of Intention business seems really simple. Too hokey to work. I don't know how you could possibly get all that from what we do here at the El. I think this all sounds like you came in here with this stuff in your head and you simply made the things you found here fit your ideas."

"Jack. Of course I came in here with the *basic* concepts in my head. That's what I study, that's what I do for a living. But, believe me, the Four P's and the Eye of Intention grew directly out of my observances of you and Dianne, your employees, and the El's customers. And you *do* use these principles. Every day. Tell me. How did things work out between you and George?"

Jack looks over at the line of people waiting for their afternoon coffee and replays his final conversation with George.

~ ~

"I'm tired, Jack. I just don't seem to care anymore," *Jack's longtime barista George says. "I like the customers and I don't have any problem with you or the work itself, but I just don't feel like getting up and coming to work anymore. You know, what's really bad is that I think it's starting to affect how I deal with the customers. I've noticed that several people who used to stop in have started walking past and going into Nordstrom's café instead. I'm afraid if I continue like this, I'll hurt the business. I think I'm going to have to give it up. At least for a while."*

The meeting George had requested wasn't going at all like Jack had envisioned. No screaming, no anxiety, no accusations, no recriminations. Jack wasn't sure that if the roles were reversed that he would be handling it as well as George was.

"George, I'm sorry things have come to this, but if you don't feel you're doing your best and you don't see any other way around it, I agree that taking a break is probably a good thing. If I had to guess, I'd say you were starting to get out of balance. Life shouldn't be all work and no play. And ever since you've been opening, you've been working six days a week. All that devotion and loyalty has been great for the business and for me, but I think maybe we overdid it. In hindsight, I don't think I should have let you work so much. I should have made you take a day off."

"Maybe so, but I would have fought you if you'd tried to make me stay away," George says. *"I love this place and I love the customers. I just think it's time for me to do something different anyway. You always said you never expected anyone to work here forever. I don't know how you keep going."*

~ ~

"Sounds like you worked everything out," Carol says, "and that George really took responsibility for his actions."

Jack nods. "That's the way it may have ended up, but believe me it didn't start out that way. We talked about it three times today. Or, at least, we tried to. What was really happening was that neither one of us wanted to deal with it. We were both trying to avoid conflict. Eventually, I guess, we both got down to the real issue—what was George's, I almost hate to say this, but what was George's *intention*."

"And once that became clear?" Carol asks.

"Once that was clear, then it was easier for each of us to talk about what should be done about the problem."

"And what was that?"

"George gave us two weeks' notice and I gave him six months to think about what he wants to do. If he decides to come back, I've promised to help him achieve his goals. Whatever they may be."

"See?" Carol says. "You knew what to do all along."

"Maybe you're right about the Four P's thing. But if it's that easy, why am I not seeing it?"

"Maybe because you're living it. It's easier for me because I can walk in here with the unprejudiced eyes of an impartial observer and see what's really going on."

"So, let's say you're right about all this. I still don't see how it can work for me."

"It's already worked once, Jack. It'll work again."

"I'm not so sure."

"Well, that's the beauty of it—you get to decide. You may be in a tough marketplace, but you have the ingredients to make it. Tell you what. You spend some time, review your intentions, and then make a conscious effort to apply the Four P's again. You do that, and after six weeks I'll stop in and see how you're doing. How's that sound?"

"I'm not sure it will work, but I want it to."

"See, you're already working on your intentions."

"OK. I guess I hired you for a reason. I'll give it a try."

"See you in six weeks."

EPILOGUE
Six Weeks Later

Pine Street and Fourth Avenue
Downtown Seattle
10:00 A.M.

The sun is shining in a cloudless sky and it hasn't rained in four days. In Seattle, that's considered near-drought conditions. The temperature is in the upper 60s, lower 70s; warm enough to be out and about, cool enough to want a cup of coffee in your hand.

Jack Hartman is sitting on a bench across from The El Espresso, a ristretto steaming in his hands.

His friend, Jim Howse, is sitting next to him. It's the first time they've had a serious conversation in nearly six weeks.

"You look rested; no circles under your eyes. You're full of energy. You're a different man, Jim. What happened?"

"You know, Jack, it's really wild. I couldn't get out of my head what you said about how you'd run my business. I took it to heart and began to think about everything I did and why. One of the things I discovered was that I didn't trust my employees at all—I thought of them as the enemy, not as allies. Not as people who could help me make my business work. And I wasn't all that fond of my customers, either. I saw that my people and I had let our customer service slip—and—in the bar biz, that's the beginning of the end. People can get a drink and a sandwich lots of places. What *we* wanted was not only to keep the cash register ringing but to have them come back every day! The amount of distrust the staff had

for each other was obvious to the customers and it was driving away people who would have liked to become regulars. Between all that and my checking up on people all the time, I realized I wasn't trying to succeed, I was trying not to fail."

"I know what you mean. So what did you do?"

"Well, I decided to do what you said. I sat down with Debbe, my night manager, and asked her what she thought our place *should* be, you know, what kind of bar we wanted. Then I asked her to suggest some ways to improve the business. It was hard to let go, but I told her I thought her ideas sounded great and that she should go ahead and put them in place. Then I stopped coming in at three in the morning."

"How did that go? Did you see things get better right away?"

"Well . . . hardly. It took almost a month—but I kept at it, and eventually the staff started to pick up on it. They saw how well Debbe and I were getting along and that I was letting her do her own thing. Now they're starting to come up with ideas of their own. We're just beginning to try some of them out and, I have to admit, things are going great. Our revenues are up and we seem to be getting more customers—and keeping the ones we get. From what I can tell our profits are way up. Best of all, we're getting along fine. And I'm sleeping more. I feel like a new man—and I have you to thank."

"That's great, Jim. I'm glad for you! Seeing you look so good and hearing how well things are going for your business is—well—what *I* needed to hear, too. But I didn't really tell you anything you didn't already know. I just could see it easier because I wasn't standing in the middle of it like you were. It's sort of the same thing that happened to me with my business consultant."

"Oh, yeah. That's right. I forgot about that. Whatever she told you must have worked. Things here seem to be going great, too. Lately, I'm starting to see longer lines, like you used to have before that dot-com moved out. What'd she tell you?"

"Essentially, she told me the same things I told you. I think, like you, I probably knew most of it before; I just wasn't focusing on it anymore."

"How did you get back into focus, then?"

"Well, I went back to basics, things I did when I started. I brought back the chalkboard and started asking a question of the day every day again. That got people talking with me and with each other. Some of them even suggested ideas for the next day's question. I held weekly contests, which we'd stopped doing a while back, and we started taking free coffee to a different office every day. And I've started writing out a formal training manual, putting in writing all the things I've learned over the years. Plus the things that Carol helped me remember about how to run a business, and what it was that made me want to be in business for myself in the first place."

"Wow! You sound like it's really coming together for you."

"Yeah. You know, it's funny, Jim, but I guess I'd forgotten how much I really do love what I do.

Oh, I may not love it all the time, and I may question certain things, kind of like George did before
he left. But seeing things from the outside, like
Carol saw it? Man. That made all the difference.
You know how much hard work running a business is. It demands a huge amount of energy,
from me *and* from my employees. And I'd been
wondering about my passion. My commitment.
Would I be able to get it back?

"Once I looked back at what I really wanted
and recommitted to what Carol calls the
Four P's, I knew I'd be able to keep it up over
the long haul. Now, I feel like I have a new
lease on my business. And my life. I feel totally
reenergized."

"Four pees? I only know one kind of—"

"Get your mind out of the gutter! Carol says a
business succeeds on four main factors: There's
Passion, that's how much you care about what
you're doing. People, the way you pick your staff
and get them ready to work, and the way you set
things up so you attract the customers you really
want. Personal, how you turn your staff and

your customers into friends,
people who belong with you.
And Product, of course, that
what you're selling is worth
buying. So that's the 'Four P's'—
and Passion is where it starts."

"You really do have your passion
back, Jack. Maybe I should sit down
with Carol next time she's in town. It sounds like
it would be worth it."

"It would be, but it sounds like you're getting
things under control all by yourself."

"Yeah—but, like you said, somebody outside your
business can see what you're doing easier than
you can. I figure if she's helped you, I could learn
a thing or two myself."

"Funny you should say that, because I'm expecting her this afternoon. Give me your card and I'll
give it to her when she comes."

"Thanks, Jack. I gotta go. Got a meeting with
Danny—he's my day manager—says he wants to

talk to me about how to punch up our lunch business. Why don't you stop by later and let me buy you a drink. I owe you at least one."

"My pleasure. See you."

Jack sips the rest of his ristretto. As he thinks about his conversation with Jim, he suddenly realizes he's eager to see Carol again. Not only because his business is booming again and he wants to tell her about it, but also because he wants to talk to her about how he's helped Jim improve his business using the universal truths of the Four P's and the Eye of Intention.

By the time Carol Wisdom walks up, Jack is more than ready.

"Hey, Carol. Am I ever glad to see you. Let me pull you a latte and we'll sit down and talk. And you can turn on your tape recorder. I've got so much to tell you that you could write a book."

A PAGE FROM CAROL WISDOM'S NOTES
The Four Principles for Running a Business in Good Times or Bad

PASSION, PEOPLE, PERSONAL, PRODUCT—
A RECIPE FOR LIFE AND WORK
*Pour some of each into your work and working
relationships to experience satisfaction and
success in all that you do*

It's All About Passion

- Do what you love and you won't work another day in your life.
- Listen to your heart and discover your personal source for positive energy.
- Build your work around your passion.
- Pursue a vision—blend your work and play.
- Share it generously with others.
- Create a climate where everybody can freely express their own passion.
- It's about what you're doing being a natural extension of yourself.

Make It Happen with People

- Look for people who share your values.
- Abandon the use of fear and force in relationships.
- Clearly communicate and develop shared expectations.
- Honor and uplift all the individuals you deal with and recognize their contributions.
- Bring the best of your whole self to work each day.

- Assume the positive—trust yourself and extend trust to others.
- Help others to succeed.
- Have few rules and no secrets.
- Create the stage for every employee to receive a standing ovation daily.

You've Gotta Make It Personal
- Practice simple gestures of courtesy.
- Be authentic and well intentioned in all situations.
- Initiate positive interaction.
- Open the door and go beyond the transaction—be generous.
- Act like an owner and host.
- Make it an experience—treat everyone as unique and valued.
- It's about engaging not just your hands but your head and your heart in your work.

Product Is the Foundation
- Be as passionate about your product as you are about the people.

- Find little ways to differentiate and delight.
- Listen to the customer.
- Treat every interaction as the first and best.
- Create confidence with consistency.
- Earn a reputation for having a product that your customers cannot stop talking about.

The Eye of Intention
- Be clear about how you define your success.
- Envision what you want your relationship with your work to be.
- Be confident in pursuing your hopes, dreams, and aspirations.
- Seek to understand and respect the intentions of others.
- Make positive choices as opportunities present themselves.
- Use your intentions to measure the rightness of your direction.

DISCUSSION QUESTIONS
Applying the Four P's to Your Work Experiences

The following questions are designed to help you understand your relationship to work. Your answers should give you insight into your current position and lead you to discover what you need to do to make the changes that will help you achieve your intentions.

The questions are divided by chapters and sub-divided for individual or workgroup situations.

Enjoy the conversation.

CHAPTER ONE: PASSION

Individual

- Life is too much fun and too short to sleep through. Do you have passion for what you do? If not, why not?
- What could you do to find that passion and bring it with you each and every day?
- Do other people feel or experience your passion through your work?
- Can you sustain your passion over time?
- If you find your passion fading, how do you re-ignite it?

Workgroup

- Rather than wait for their customers to develop a passion for The El Espresso, Jack and Dianne decided to do things to generate that passion in their customers. How can you apply this concept to your work and working relationships?
- As a supervisor, how can you facilitate the expression of passion?
- What does it mean to work for a passionate company? Can passion and profits coexist

harmoniously? Is passion valued in organizations today?

- How big a role does passion play in your own organization? Who shows it regularly? How else does it manifest itself? Are the customers aware of it? What is standing in the way?
- How can passion be ignited in a company during difficult times? Is it related to motivation? How?
- What were the guiding principles of your own organization? Are they still in place? Do the employees know of them?
- The El Espresso is undergoing a business downturn. Have you experienced something similar in your career? How did management deal with it? Was that an effective solution? Why or why not?

CHAPTER TWO: PEOPLE

Individual

- What kind of people do you have working for you or with you?
- What kind of person are you?
- Are your customers the right ones?

- Have you been selective in choosing them
  and have you adequately prepared to serve
  them well?
- Have you created enduring relationships with
  those you serve and with whom you work?
- What reputation are you working on earning?
  With your coworkers? With your supervisor?
  With your customers?
- Do you feel like your work life and personal
  life are in balance? If not, why not? If not, how
  can you achieve that balance?

Workgroup

- Jack Hartman speculated about whether
  his business would be viable without the employees. How important are people in your
  organization?
- Do the employees feel valued by management?
  Why or why not?
- Several of Jack's employees regard working at
  The El Espresso as being about more than the
  money. Is that true for you? Does your own
  organization reward employees in ways beyond
  their paychecks? Does it motivate them?

- Are there other ways you would like your company to express appreciation to its employees?
- One of Jack's customers talked about not trusting the employees who work at his bar. What role do you think trust and mistrust play in how employees behave in their day-to-day jobs? What do you think management could do to demonstrate trust?
- One of Jack's employees talked about losing his passion for the job. What could Jack have done to salvage an employee like George? Is it natural for someone to develop job burnout over time? Why or why not?

CHAPTER THREE: PERSONAL

Individual

- Everybody wants to be a regular somewhere. Are you treating your customers like your friends? Do you know their names? The names of their family members? What they like to do when they're not at work? Can you say the same for your employees or coworkers?
- Do you make a meaningful connection with your customers and coworkers each and every

day? Have you seen your efforts result in the creation of community?

- What do you do to get your customers involved?
- Jack recalled working in a theme park where the employees referred to the customers as "animals." How do you talk about your customers? How does that affect the way you treat them?
- Sally Norton, a loyal El customer, found her life mate standing in line buying his morning cup of coffee. Do you have any positive customer stories to share that were a direct result of the community created by you or your company?

Workgroup

- Jack talks about how important it is for employees to engage with customers. How important do you think customer loyalty is for your organization? Can you think of ways that your organization could do more to encourage customer engagement and loyalty?
- One of The El Espresso's customers talked about the seriousness and playfulness of the

staff there. Is your own workplace too serious? Too playful? Can management encourage a good balance between the two? How?

- Carol Wisdom talked about research indicating that employee loyalty translates into customer loyalty. Do you agree? How would improved employee morale in your own organization make a difference in customer retention?

- Loyalty to The El Espresso is the foremost trait of its customers. Is loyalty the foremost trait of your customers? If not, why not?

- For Jack Hartman, the way he brings himself to work every day makes a major difference in how the day will ultimately turn out. Do you agree? How can you adapt your own attitude so that you arrive ready to have a good day rather than a difficult one?

- Several customers talked about how they like being greeted by name and feeling part of the family. What does your organization do to make customers feel special? What new technologies can larger companies employ to treat their customers like family?

- One of the customers talked about the importance of treating people right. What does that mean in your organization? Is it taught? Is it stressed? Are people empowered to determine what constitutes treating customers right? What could your company do to apply some of the lessons that have worked so well for The El Espresso?

- One customer said he has heard The El Espresso is experiencing difficult times. Has your own company gone through a similar experience? How were the employees informed? How were the customers informed? Evaluate the process and describe the results.

- Another customer said that at the El the customer is first and service is king. In your organization, what is first? What is king?

CHAPTER FOUR: PRODUCT

Individual

- None of the other P's can save a bad product. Do you pay attention to the quality of what you make? What you serve? How you perform?

- Does your product represent who you are to the world?

- Have you created an environment where consistent product excellence can be sustained? How do you go about making changes to popular products and still maintain customer loyalty?

Workgroup

- Over the years The El Espresso spent time and money creating the best product available. What has your company done to make a better product or service? How are they telling your customers about it?
- Jack Hartman said consistency is one of the hallmarks of a good product. Do you agree? How does a company maintain the quality for which it has become known?
- Carol said that customers' feelings about The El Espresso's coffee have taken on mythic proportions: in their mind there is no coffee like the El's. Has your product or service attained mythic proportions in your customers' minds? If not, what do you need to do to make that happen?
- One customer said that good service cannot rescue a bad product, but bad service can destroy a good product. Do you agree? Can you think of examples of that happening in the business world in your own employment history?

- Pressure for cost cutting is inevitable in any business and so are price increases. Jack said he would rather raise prices than sacrifice quality with a poorer bean. How does a company balance this issue? How should it communicate price increases to its customers?

- Carol counseled Jack on the importance of getting the fundamentals right. In *your* business, what are the fundamentals? How does management convey the importance of getting these right to the employees? Is management concentrating on the *right* fundamentals?

- Carol described a distinct correlation between the way employees see their company's product or service and the level of their devotion to it. Do you agree? Have you seen instances where the employees actually created a better product or service because of the way they viewed that product or service? What could management do to encourage that behavior?

- Successful businesses are those whose employees take ownership, accountability, and responsibility for their actions and for product quality. Using this definition, is your company a success?

CHAPTER FIVE: INTENTIONS

Individual

- *Intention* is a fancy word for *plan*. Do you have a plan for your life? Do you know where you want to go? Who you want to be?
- Success is personal and relative. How do you define success for yourself? Is your job a good fit with that definition?
- Can you boast that you love what you do? If not, what kind of work should you be doing to engender this kind of feeling? How could you change your existing work or your attitude toward it to make it something you love?
- Can you describe your intentions regarding what you want to get from your work? What you want to bring to it?

Workgroup

- Carol talked about the importance of having a strategic plan for any business, large or small. Plans allow businesses to evaluate opportunities. Describe what your company intends to be.

- Does your company have a clearly stated mission? Describe and discuss it.
- What are the values of your company? Does everyone in your company share the same values? If not, why not? Should they?
- Is there a vision for a future state that energizes employees and customers alike? What aspect of that future aligns with your personal intentions? How can you help your organization achieve that future?
- When Jack took advantage of the opportunity to expand his business, he was not pleased with the results. Why did he feel like that? How would you feel if your company were faced with the same opportunity? What are some viable alternatives to expansion for you and your company?

CHAPTER SIX: THE FOUR P'S

Individual and Group Work

- How well has your own company adapted its own version of the Four P's? What actions can you take to ensure the Four P's are incorporated in your own day-to-day work?

- What would some of the benefits be to you if your company were successful in applying the Four P's to your business? Would there be any costs?
- Describe the reputation you'd like your business to have in the community. Is that vision consistent with the current reality? Why or why not?
- Carol described the Four P's as universal, saying that they can be applied in any size business in any kind of industry. Do you agree? Why or why not?
- What can you do *today* to make work more fun for you and more profitable for your company?

APPENDIX
Caffeine Facts

A Short History of Coffee Through the Ages

600	Coffee makes its migration from Ethiopia to Arabia.
1000	The philosopher Avicenna first describes the medicinal qualities of coffee, which he refers to as bunchum.
1300	Islamic monks brew qawha, a blend of hot water and roasted coffee beans.
1453	Sultan Selim I introduces coffee to Constantinople. Turkish law makes

it legal for a woman to divorce
her husband if he fails to provide her
with her daily quota of coffee.

1500   Coffee use spreads to Mecca and
Medina.

1511   Khair Beg, the corrupt governor of
Mecca, tries to ban coffee for fear
that its influence might foster oppo-
sition to his rule. The sultan sends
word that coffee is sacred and has
the governor executed.

1600   Baba Budan, a Moslem pilgrim,
introduces coffee to southern India.

1607   Captain John Smith helps to found
the colony of Virginia at Jamestown.
It is widely believed that he introduced coffee to North America.

1616   Coffee is brought from Mocha to
Holland.

1645   The first coffee house opens in Venice.

1652   The first coffee house opens in
Oxford, England.

1658   The Dutch begin cultivating coffee in
Ceylon (Sri Lanka).

1668	Coffee replaces beer as New York City's favorite breakfast beverage.
	Edward Lloyd's coffee house opens in England and is frequented by merchants and maritime insurance agents. Eventually it becomes Lloyd's of London, the best-known insurance company in the world.
1669	Coffee catches on in Paris when a Turkish ambassador spends a year in the court of Louis XIV.
1674	The Women's Petition Against Coffee is introduced in London.
1675	King Charles II orders all London coffee houses closed, calling them places of sedition.
1679	Marseilles physicians try to discredit coffee, claiming it is harmful to health.
1689	The first enduring Parisian coffee house, Cafe de Procope, opens.
1696	The King's Arms, New York's first coffee house, opens.
1706	The first samples of coffee grown in Java are brought back to Amsterdam.

1713	A coffee plant, raised from a seed of the Java samples, is presented by the Dutch to Louis XIV and maintained in the Jardin des Plantes in Paris.
1720	The still-enduring Caffe Florian opens in Florence.
1721	Germany's first coffee house opens in Berlin.
1723	Gabriel de Clieu brings a coffee seedling from France to Martinique.
1730	The English bring coffee cultivation to Brazil.
1732	Bach composes "The Coffee Cantata," parodying the German paranoia over coffee's growing popularity.
1773	The Boston Tea Party makes drinking coffee a patriotic duty in America.
1777	Prussia's Frederick the Great issues a manifesto denouncing coffee in favor of the national drink, beer.
1809	The first coffee imported from Brazil arrives in Salem, Massachusetts.
1869	Coffee leaf rust appears in Ceylon. Within ten years, the disease

destroys most of the plantations
in India, Ceylon, and other parts
of Asia.

1873   The first successful national brand
of packaged roast coffee, Ariosa, is
marketed by John Arbuckle.

1882   The New York Coffee Exchange commences business.

1886   Former wholesale grocer Joel Cheek
names his popular coffee blend
"Maxwell House" after the hotel in
Nashville, Tennessee, where it is
served.

1904   The modern espresso machine is
invented by Fernando Illy.

1906   Brazil withholds some coffee from
the world market in an attempt to
boost global prices.

1911   American coffee roasters organize
into a national association, the
precursor to the National Coffee
Association.

1928   The Colombian Coffee Federation is
established.

1938	Nestlé technicians in Brazil invent Nescafé, the first commercially successful instant coffee.
1942	U.S. troops bring freeze-dried Maxwell House instant coffee to a global audience. Back home, widespread hoarding leads to coffee rationing.
1946	In Italy, Achilles Gaggia perfects his espresso machine. Cappuccino is named for the resemblance of its color to the robes of the Capuchin monks.
1959	Juan Valdez becomes the face of Colombian coffee.
1962	Peak in American per-capita coffee consumption—more than three cups a day.
1964	First Tim Horton's opens in Hamilton, Ontario.
1971	First Starbucks opens in Seattle, selling roasted coffee beans.
1973	First fair-trade coffee is imported to Europe from Guatemala.
1975	Global coffee prices rise dramatically after Brazil suffers a severe frost.

Second Cup makes its debut in Canada.

1980   The world's first espresso cart commences business under the Monorail in Seattle.

1989   International Coffee Agreement collapses as world prices drop to an historic low.

early 1990s   Specialty coffee catches on in the United States.

mid-1990s   Organic coffee becomes the fastest-growing segment of the specialty coffee industry.

1997   Tim Horton's introduces first specialty coffees, English Toffee and French Vanilla cappuccinos.

1998   Starbucks approaches 2,000 U.S. outlets, with as many planned for Asia and Europe.

1999   A tiny espresso counter, the basis for this book, becomes the sole downtown Seattle-based business to remain open during the World Trade Organization riots.

Acknowledgments

Without the cooperation, hospitality, magnanimity, and leadership abilities of our coffee-loving sources, this book could not have been written. Though we will not name them, our deepest appreciation and admiration go to them, their employees, and their customers. We also thank them for turning us on to the best cup of coffee in Seattle.

Leslie would like to thank Charles for inviting her to share in the fun of telling the story of a healthy organization and its aspiring individuals. To Randy Martin for being my partner, my foil,

145

my wordsmith, and my editor. To Susan Martin for the necessary but tedious work of copyediting. To Mike Agrippe and Bill Wilkins, members of the Catalyst Consulting Group team, for their constant support and presence. And to all of you who have the vision and passion to try new things and improve your work.

Charles would like to thank the thousands of business owners, managers, and employees who are living a variation of this story, unheralded, in companies and organizations across the country and around the world. You are an inspiration to us all. Charles would also like to thank a few people who offered their advice and encouragement during the time the book was percolating, most especially Jerry Austin, Matt Barnes, Lisa Biernbaum, Linda Chaput, Marilyn Dahl, Brooke Gilbert, Kathy Gilligan, Teri Kieffer, Will Lippincott, Barbara Monteiro, and Patrick Orton.

The Jossey-Bass/Wiley family has served as an amazing support system during the writing of this book, and we would like to thank Debra Hunter, Cedric Crocker, Erik Thrasher, Todd Berman, Mary Garrett, Hilary Powers, Karen Warner, and

~ Beans ~

Bernadette Walter at Jossey-Bass (as well as Jennifer Johnson at Wiley) for their unbridled and unwavering enthusiasm for this simple but illuminating story. Susan Williams was an early champion of the book and we thank her, particularly, for being our advocate, editor, and friend. She is a living testament to how valuable a role an editor plays in the development of a book. There is not another publisher, in our experience, as author-friendly as Jossey-Bass/Wiley. We celebrate our experience with them every day of our lives.

About the Authors

Leslie A. Yerkes: Self-Proclaimed Sherpa Guide

Leslie's measure of her success as a business leader and consultant is that she applies to herself first all the consulting principles in which she engages her clients. In her work as an organizational development and change management consultant, her goal is not to be positioned as an expert but rather as a trusted adviser. Leslie earned her M.S. in organizational development at Case Western Reserve University after graduating from Wittenberg University with a B.A. cum laude. She founded Catalyst Consulting Group

Inc. in 1987. Her philosophy is simple: People are basically good, well intentioned, courageous, and able to learn. Her job is to provide a framework in which they can draw on their own inner resources to find creative solutions.

In many ways, Leslie is a paradox. She was born an old soul who, while in her early mid-life, maintains a perpetual state of Peter Pan—gotta fight, gotta fly, gotta crow. She is a fountain of ideas, but concerned with the smallest detail. Her comfort for risk taking is extreme yet, regarding her role in life and her concern for others, she is overly responsible. She relishes rituals and symbolism, yet cannot resist a spontaneous adventure.

Leslie values leadership, loyalty, and trust in relationships.

Some of her role models include Mother Teresa, Albert Einstein, Amelia Earhart, Viktor Frankl, Eleanor Roosevelt, Joseph Campbell, and Click and Clack the Tappet Brothers.

She is a voracious learner and places high value on her own journey of discovery.

Leslie has a passion for finding and telling stories of healthy organizations. Her published works include *301 Ways to Have Fun at Work,* and *Fun Works: Creating Places Where People Love to Work.* She is a contributor to *Business: The Ultimate Resource.*

Leslie lives and works in Cleveland, Ohio. When she plays she likes to play in Australia and Europe. Her list of favorite play includes fly-fishing, scuba diving, cattle drives, community theater, swimming with dolphins, and time spent with family and friends.

Charles R. Decker

Charles has been involved with business and professional publishing for more than twenty years. As director of Doubleday's *Executive Program* book club, he previewed more than fifteen hundred business manuscripts a year for potential inclusion in the club.

He received numerous accolades for his launch of the Business Literacy 2000 program during that time, which continues to foster group reading in

corporations across America and around the
world. The former president and publisher of
Berrett-Koehler Communications in San Francisco, most recently he was the senior editor
responsible for merchandising the Professional
and Technical bookstore at Amazon.com in
Seattle. Charles was one of the founding partners
of Acumentum Inc., a digital publisher based in
New York and San Francisco.

Charles is currently at work on a second book
celebrating another company that espouses
humanitarian management.

Contact Page

The following support materials are currently available to assist you in energizing your organization:

A video program based on the book *Beans: Four Principles for Running a Business in Good Times or Bad* is available for purchase or rental through

Star Thrower Distribution
26 E. Exchange Street
St. Paul, Minnesota 55101
800-242-3220
info@starthrower.com

Custom Keynote Address: Energize your organization with an interactive presentation that will enliven the power of the Four P's and teach you to see your success through the Eye of Intention.

To learn more about how to create a culture infused with the Four P's, please contact us at

Catalyst Consulting Group Inc.
1111 Chester Avenue
Cleveland, Ohio 44114
216-241-3939
216-241-3977 fax
fun@catalystconsulting.net
http://www.changeisfun.com
http://www.beansthebook.com

We would love to hear your stories of how your organization has applied the Four P's.